ECOLOGY AND QUALITY OF LIFE IN URBAN SLUMS

About the Authors

Dr. (Mrs.) Rekha Sinha *(b. 1958)* is currently Professor of Psychology, T.M. Bhagalpur University, Bhagalpur. She has contributed more than 20 research papers to the reputed national and international journals of Psychology and other social-sciences. She has completed two UGC Major Research Projects and has also authored one book, entitled : Organised and Disorganised Personality : A Comparative Study. Organizational, Industrial & Environmental Psychology are the areas of her interest in research

Dr. U.P. Sinha *(b. 1956)* is Professor of Economics, T.M. Bhagalpur University, Bhagalpur. He has authored many books including Planned Development of Resources in a Developing Region (1985), Socio-Economic Dimensions of Integrated Development in India (1991) and IRDP for Weaker Sections (1996). He is editing 'Journal of Economic Issues' since 2000 published by Planning Forum, and Anga Economic Society, University Department of Economics, T.M. Bhagalpur University, Bhagalpur. He has also completed two UGC Major Research Projects and contributed more than 50 research papers to reputed national and international journals of Economics and other social-sciences. Micro-level planning and the regional economics are the areas of his interest and research.

ECOLOGY AND QUALITY OF LIFE IN URBAN SLUMS

An Empirical Study

Rekha Sinha
University Professor,
Department of Psychology
T.M. Bhagalpur University
Bhagalpur

&

U.P. Sinha
University Professor,
Department of Economics
T.M. Bhagalpur University
Bhagalpur

CONCEPT PUBLISHING COMPANY, NEW DELHI-110059

Cataloging in Publication Data—DK
Courtesy: D.K. Agencies (P) Ltd. <docinfo@dkagencies.com>

Sinha, Rekha, 1958-
Ecology and quality of life in urban slums : an empirical study / Rekha Sinha & U.P. Sinha.
p. cm.
Study conducted at Munger and Bhagalpur cities of Bihar, India.
Includes bibliographical references (p.)
Includes index.
ISBN 8180693732

1. Urban ecology—India—Munger. 2. Urban ecology—India—Bhagalpur. 3. Quality of life—India—Munger. 4. Quality of life—India—Bhagalpur. 5. Slums—India—Munger. 6. Slums—India—Bhagalpur. I. Sinha, U. P., 1956-, joint author. II. Title.

DDC 307.760 954 123 22

ISBN : 81-8069-373-2 (HB)

First Published 2007

Published and Printed by
Ashok Kumar Mittal
Concept Publishing Company
A/15-16, Commercial Block, Mohan Garden
New Delhi-110059 (India)

Phones : 25351460, 25351794
Fax : 091-11-25357103
Email : publishing@conceptpub.com

FOREWORD

The quintessence of Ecology is a sort of feasible and necessary harmony between men and nature. The 'ecology movement' puts stress on the interdependence of living things. It also spells out that the resources must be directed towards the settings in which people live and work and interact with each other so that tension may be reduced and healthy conditions are promoted. These movements are, joined and supported by the consumer movement, which encourage users of human services to organize and become well informed in order to hold the provider of services accountable for the quality of their services. It attempts to raise consciousness about the myths that have made services so hard for citizens or consumers to influence.

Society should be prepared to regard quality of life processes integrated with the earth ecosystems. We have not only to solve the existing environmental problems but to forecast future ones. We have at the same time to educate men to new lifestyles whether they are for natural or artificial habitats. Indeed, there has to be all round environmental revolution as stated by Max Nicholson. Economists, psychologists, sociologists and naturalists have to face the most pressing environmental problems and challenges together.

Environment-behaviour research has gathered momentum during the last three decades (Stokols, 1997), environmental psychologists, ecological psychologists, behaviour ecologists and organizational psychologists have been time and again, emphasizing the impact of ecological constraints on human behaviour. Some of them relate their theoretical framework to urban sociology. The theory of 'Psychic Overload' assumes that residence in a densely populated area leads to more perceptual stimulation from exposure to other people and their by products like noise pollution and personal space problems. As a result, adaptations are required to screen out less desirable inputs. But these adaptations become costly. The results at the social level are high level of pathology, while at the individual level, a cultural lifestyle develops that serves to isolate the individual from unwanted inputs (Simmel, 1989; Milgram, 1980; Desor, 1987; Baum and Valins, 1993; Shered, 1994).

Some other refer to the concept of personal space. People naturally need personal territories and, if they do not get it, they feel frustrated. This generates feelings of anxiety. Urban residential life leads to stress (Sommer, 1989; Evans & Howard 1996; Hall, 1996). As such, the present study seems essential in order to contain the anxiety level of urban residents and their plans to spend a good life.

Along with 'Boom town' studies, social scientists, mental health professionals and social impact assessors have time and again put emphasis on understanding urban slum dwellers and their ecological constraints. A number of psycho-social conditions such as crowding, personal space, stress, adaptation and other socio-economic factors influence the lifestyle of slum dwellers in different part of the country. Rapid urbanization and industrialization have resulted in the growth of slums. These are overcrowded shabby living places. Most of the inhabitants are industrial workers, daily wage earners, and other indigent people. Dr. R.K. Mukherjee a leading sociologist has summed up the situation thus "In the thousand slums of India's industrial centres, manhood is unquestionably brutalized, women dishonoured, a childhood is poisoned at its very source".

Let us accept the reality that the slums are there and they will continue to exist, particularly, in underdeveloped third world countries like that of ours. One should give serious thought to the problems and devise certain strategies to reduce the tension, conflicts and low quality of life experienced by the slum dwellers. One of the alternatives is to develop leadership among slum dwellers, so that they understand, analyse and comprehend their own problems. Their participation should be assured in the action programmes undertaken for the betterment of the slums. Participatory Research Approach (PRA) should be given weightage. In such a situation the present study helps in a leadership training programme for the slums. The contribution by Dr. (Mrs.) Rekha Sinha and Dr. Udai P. Sinha are an important step in this direction. I hope that this would stimulate debate and discussion on this fundamental issues.

The book has been designed to undertake the upgradation of slums and squatter settlements in the cities of Munger and Bhagalpur with a view to highlight the socio-economic life of the urban society in terms of environmental pollution which has been developing a sense of insecurity in urban areas not only for the urban authorities but also for the scholars, town planners, administrator and society in general.

This book is commendable with the hope that the growing social and ecological disintegration would be halted and it would provide every opportunity for the economic progress and better quality of life of the people.

U.P. Singh
Former Vice-Chancellor
S.K.M. University, Dumka
Jharkhand

Date : 21-05-06

PREFACE

Urban life in the cities of Munger and Bhagalpur has been considered as birds feather which looks quite beautiful but unfortunately its growth and development is parasitic as it depends on the surrounding zone of influence for food, vegetable and the supplies of milk and consumers to run the shops in the market. Although, the proverb 'rural poverty and urban misery' is quite famous and it is quite true in case of the cities of Munger and Bhagalpur of the Anga Plain where Angika dialect is spoken.

The objective of this research encompasses almost all aspects of urban life e.g. living conditions, food habit, psychological behaviour, dress material, ornaments used, types of recreation, musical instruments used, arts adopted, theatre performed, cinema houses along with the levels of literacy, political life, caste conflict and marketing environment, etc. Recently, it has been observed that urban life is changing fast due to the ever increasing population, cultural assimilation of people and the introduction of telephone, mobile, computer, car and the use of internet have really revolutionized the urban life of people.

Chapter one deals with the introductory background of quality of life investigation with special reference to the cities of Munger and Bhagalpur. In this chapter delineations have been made regarding meaning and scope, review of past literature, conceptual background, methods of study, sources of data, hypothesis testing and geographical personality of the area under investigation.

In second chapter delineations have been made regarding explaining the ecological conditions of the urban centres of Munger and Bhagalpur in terms of relief feature, climatic conditions, land-use patterns, resource make up of the region along with analyzing the demographic characteristics.

The third chapter is on review of conceptual framework of quality of life based on financial, cultural and caste differentiation of people. The fourth chapter in on types and patterns of urban life in relation to income group, caste and religious factors and political scenario of urban peopie of these two cities.

The fifth chapter is on measuring the levels of quality of life in relation to the average condition received through fieldwork. The sixth chapter has been devoted to slums and squatters found in the cities of Munger and Bhagalpur. This is the area of problems of poverty, misery, slum development, theft, road holds up, burglary, flood and vice of the underworld's which are rampant. Among the prospects we may hope for the better life, planned development of economy and houses, construction of bridge across the Ganga and respite from the diseases and the control of crime as population is increasing day by day.

The seventh chapter is on sample study at family, occupation, income, caste and various processes of urban life have been considered. The eighth chapter is devoted to infrastructural development in the cities of Munger and Bhagalpur in terms of road network, housing, water and electricity supplies and the development of educational institutions.

The ninth chapter is devoted to the discussion of material and child health in the slum areas of Munger and Bhagalpur in particular.

The tenth chapter is on problems and planning of quality of life both short-term and long-term issues. The chapter is based on result obtained from topographical sheets, aerial photograph and satellite imageries for the cities of Munger and Bhagalpur as all these have the capacity to give us synoptic view of the quality of life found in the urban area. In the last eleventh chapter summary and conclusion of the entire book have been presented in brief. At the end the list of books and journals has been given for further reading.

The use of maps, figures and diagrams will illustrate the problems that have exercised the minds of scholars, researchers and town planners in this wide ranging subject.

Bhagalpur
14-01-2006

Rekha Sinha
U.P. Sinha

ACKNOWLEDGEMENTS

The conduct of field investigation is a joint endeavour and in such cases the success depends upon whole hearted co-operation of everyone involved in the preparation of the present research report. It is the devotion to the work as well as proper suggestion, guidance, moral and financial help that determine the outcome of such works.

First and foremost, we owe a deep sense of gratitude to Prof. Uday Pratap Singh, former Vice-Chancellor, S.K.M. University, Dumka, who wrote the foreword of the book.

We are extremely grateful to my teacher Dr. (Mrs.) Usha Rani Singh, University Professor & Head, Department of Psychology and Dean, Faculty of Social Sciences, T.M. Bhagalpur University, Bhagalpur who has always been a fountain of inspiration to us.

We wish to express deep sense of gratitude to R.B. Mandal, University Professor of Geography, T.M. Bhagalpur University, Bhagalpur for thought provoking suggestions and guidance.

We also express our gratefulness to Dr. V.N. Singh, Professor of Psychology and Dr. R.R.L. Das, Professor & Head of Department of Economics, T.M. Bhagalpur University, Bhagalpur for valuable suggestions and criticism.

We also owe our sincere thanks to Sri D. P. Yadava, former Deputy Education Minister, Government of India, who has rendered immense help with his personal experience, thought provoking suggestions and by providing the facility to consult his personal library.

We extend my warmest thanks to the librarians and staff of National Library, Kolkata; National Institute of Rural Development, Hyderabad; Centre for Advanced Research Institute, Shimla; Pune University Central Library, Ratan Tata Library of Delhi School of Economics and Saint Xavier Institute of Social Services, Ranchi.

We owe our sincere thanks to Sri Tribhuwan Poddar, Department of Zoology, T.M. Bhagalpur University, Bhagalpur for cartographic work, who have been very helpful to me in the completion of this Project.

Lastly, we also acknowledge our sincere thanks to Md. Reyaz who has painstakingly typed the whole report with great pain.

On the eve of Maker Sankranti,
14th January, 2006,
Bhaglapur

Rekha Sinha
U.P. Sinha

CONTENTS

LIST OF TABLES

LIST OF FIGURES

List of Graphs

1 INTRODUCTION

'Quality of life' as any other concept in social science has been defined in a number of ways. In order to know the level of living people in a given geographical area is constituted by over all consumption of housing, health, education, social status, employment, affluence, leisure hour, social security and social stability. The rapid rate of urbanization during the 20th and 21st centuries has created not only socio-economic problems but also an unprecedented concern of the physical environment degradation. Abyssal poverty, social desirability and lack of proper opportunity in rural areas forces men to migrate to urban areas. All these have made the quality of life very miserable.

Urban is an area where the majority of people are engaged in non-agricultural occupation within the command of municipal corporation or municipality. Slums are the unhygienic localities in the urban centres where congestion of houses, dump of garbage on the road side, open drains of refuge water, service latrines, lack of street lights, broken metalled or unmetalled roads and the dingy looking houses dominate the scene. Ecology is the environmental condition of people in the slum where they reside even if the area is ill-ventilated, congested and the life is miserable and struggling in nature. In such a situation mostly the poors are living in the slum because the houses are relatively cheap in comparison with other areas.

Due to alarming growth of population in the last census (2001) the Government of India has taken stock of the situation regarding quality of life of people in the cities in which 34 variables have been considered, i.e. whether the family owns a car, fan, T.V. set, radio set, electricity, motor cycle, bicycle along with their literacy, food habit, ornaments, dress material and others. We obtained data on all these items has been considered quite essential in order to know the ecological condition and quality of life of people residing in a particular locality. Quality of urban life is closely related with the social, cultural, economic, and political life of people in the region under study. Due to hum-drum reality of urban life it is difficult to identify one another because the frequent meeting is not possible along with the variations in caste, income potential, difference in or culture and the standard of living are the major causes of the variations in quality of life. Quality of life helps in knowing the living standard of people and how the situations could be improved for the better especially in the slum areas.

This study has been organized in different segments which is based on analysis of maps prepared ward-wise and the data collected from fieldwork in the slum areas of the city such as Delawarpur, Topekhana Bazar, Chhotikela-bari, Purabsarai and Murgiachak. The intensity of slum is very high because the sitting condition is absolutely in sanitary. The heaps of garbage lies here and there and the living conditions of the poor menials the labour class people are absolutely unfit for human living. Moreover, with the decline of service facilities and increase of population the slums are cropping up everywhere in the city.

These days slums have created a panic for cities development. It has been a serious issue for the town planning bodies not only in India but in Europe and North America as well. Slums are the marginal areas of cities where the poor people are illiterate, drinking water supply is miserably on lowest ebb and the vice of underworlds predominate the scene. The study of slum is meaningful for environmental modification and amelioration the problems of urban areas for providing more amenities to the ailing masses. This type of study finds ground mostly in European countries, where the city centres are the problem areas for city dwellers and people want clean air to breath. In such a situation, this study has been directly related to highlight the urban problems in a developing urban scenario of Munger and Bhagalpur.

Urban centres are places where the majority of population are engaged in non-agricultural functions and the place having municipality or notified area committee. Hence, urban life is purely artificial and nothing is natural except land, air, water and vegetation cover. In this way, urbanism is a way of life of people where every thing resembles new and designed in a new style. Modernity is the way of life and very few laggards are behind the old fashion. Urbanism provides us a society of mixed nature having place of multiple functions and nothing is well known but everything is mysterious which shrouds in mystery. The urban people are cunning and miser and hence, they never be normal in their behaviour and cheating for urbanite is a common practice.

The city life is not dichotomy to the rural living but they are complementary to each other. The variations in urban life has been noticed in terms of literacy, food habit, dress material, cultural advancement of urban areas besides the hum-drum reality of urban environment. Now in urban areas the situation are deteriorating to such a pass that people are living the city for pure environment in rural areas, because the urban area is dominated by obnoxious gases, degrading morale of people, road holds up, suicide and the dominance of slums and squatters.

Paramaters to be Considered

This thesis aims at analyzing the cultural variations of people found in the urban centres of Munger and Bhagalpur. These variations have been noticed in city structure, behaviour of people, religious affiliation, caste association, business performance, wholeselling and retailing along with the cultural traits of dance, drama, music, dress material and variations in the level of education. It also includes festivals, family planning measures and health services as well.

Objectives of Study

The purpose of this study is to assess the modernity and cultural variations found in the cities of Munger and Bhagalpur. This could be assessed properly at the time of festivals and the engagement of different cultural groups especially in entertaining the people. For example, Sanskar Bharti and others are doing well in changing the people lifestyle. This study will assess some of these aspects with special reference to the cities of Munger and Bhagalpur where the dress material and food habit are closely related with the city structure and income differentials of people.

Statement of Problem

1. Variations in caste groups and associations.
2. Variations in clan migrations.
3. Differences in religion and cult.
4. Analysis of levels of literacy, dress material, food habit, marriage customs, dance, theatre, yoga and musical performance.

5. The spatial variations of colleges, schools, industrial establishment along with wholeselling and retailing.
6. Housing designs, settlement structures, intra-city central place hierarchy and psychological traits of people has been be analyzed.

Model of Urban Life

Urban life has been designed in between arts and science of the residents of townscape along with their level of education and civilization earned by the people in terms of historical events. All these are the product in terms of historical environment. Urbanism and the quality of life of non-agricultural population makes difference in culture and lifestyle of people in the core areas of the city, middle part of the city and fringe area of the city. On the whole, we can say that all these are responsible for variations in the urban life of people in Munger and Bhagalpur urban centres. Since 1995 the quality of urban life in Munger and Bhagalpur has modified manifold due to rise in the level of education of people (Fig. 1.1).

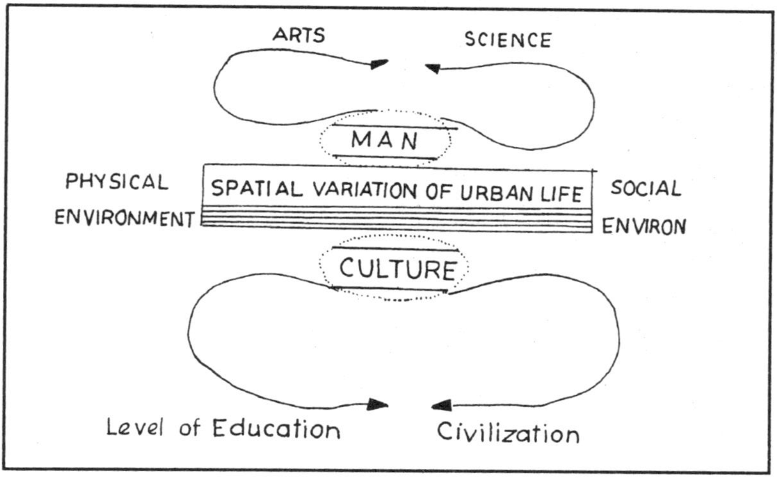

Fig. 1.1 : Model of Urban Life

Review of Past Literature

Bhatia (1975) analysed the scientific and cultural advancement made in the metropolis of Delhi, Buckley (1967) has delineated the system theory operating in urban society. Chatterjee (1964) highlighted the cultural history of Howrah port city. Dhabriya (1964) assessed the evolution of cultural landscape in the city of Udaipur. Hatt, Albert and Reiss (1963) analysed the role of society in the evolution of cities in USA. Jefferson (1931) highlighted the role of folk in the evolution of civilization. Lal (1992) considered the urban family as the base of social stratification thereby leading to variations in the urban social systems. Murphy (1969) analysed the changing urban roles in Asia in terms of traditionalism and colonialism. Pahl (1975) has made a headway towards structure and process of urban life. Reeve (1917) had considered the congestion in cities. Yadav (1992) has analysed the rise of slums along with the decline and revitalization of cities. Somehow or other all these papers are related with the delineations of urban life found in different parts of the world.

Zietsman (1992) while dealing about land for the landless in Cape city analysed that migrants to the urban centres from rural areas gets attracted due to descent living but due to unemployed they are landless, homeless, jobless and without any financial means to occupy the houses legally. Their only alternative is to erect houses on vacant land and hence illegal occupation is the only out come left. Generally squatting creates conflict with the law-abiding people, which lead to violence, a burden on the prevailing cities life.

Vooged, H. (1992) while dealing with the quality of life and images, he said that the quality of life is widely used term in practice, particularly in relation to activities like city marketing, cultural, educational, recreational, housing and infrastructure facilities available to the residents, because it cannot be assessed on terms peoples behaviour only.

Thieme, G.H. (1992) while discussing about the quality of life and mortality in Germany highlighted the indicators such as infant mortality or life expectancy at different ages which can serve as adequate measures of this important aspect of life, both in Third World and in industrial societies.

Basant Singh (1992) while giving his opinion on 'National Capital Region and Eco-Environmental Hazards' of the opinion that foresight and vision are rare qualities in public life. This observation is true in case of national capital region (NCR) too, because of its long jump urbanization; in which only take-off and landing points are considered. The larger stretch of land is ignored. Architecturally, it is not possible to give NCR as urban textures. The whole region,would emerge as an urban slum.

Saraswati Raju (1992) while assessing 'Access of the Urban Poor to Basic Amenities in Delhi, India', said that in urban areas of India 28 per cent people are poor. Not only the estimates are controversial, rather various micro-aspects of poverty generated much debate. For discussion the basic needs identified are shelter, distribution of food-grains, water supply, health care and anomalies the existing scenario has to be changed in terms of management, relaxation and flexibility in formalities and an empery towards the urban poor.

Kohal Okamoto (1992) while analysing 'the quality of life in Metropolitan suburbs of Japan' said that day-to-day life has been undergoing changes of spatio-temporal in nature. This study analyse the role of married women in the employment sector and tries to identify the obstacles that keep married women away from these activities. It has been observed that wives in households with no children or with high school students or above can easily participate in social activities. The availability of a private car again affects the quality of suburban life. The suburban environment requires that wives not only drive themselves to the shopping and recreation facilities, but also to drive their children to their activities. Thus, these wives face further fragmentation of their blocks of time. Thus the quality of life in suburban suburbs is classified in microscopic, as well as quantitative way based on the concept of time geography.

Toivo A. Mullu (1992) analysed 'The Working Life as a Part of Personal Welfare in Finland: A Regional Approach', constitutes an essential part of personal welfare. The intellectuals income gained from work in a society based on paid employment creates a socio-economic resources based upon which the other sectors of life are based. The unemployment and various changes in working life style give rise to inequality on the labour market in terms of variations in occupation and sex.

H. N. Mishra (1993) while analysing 'the quality of life in squatter settlements: A case study of Chhestpur, Allahabad' said that *Jhuggies*, *Jhopadies*, popular settlements, barrios, favelas, ranches, kampongs have become an integral part of urban life in the Third World countries. They are indicative of the basic human needs and institutional capabilities top meet the need of housing, people find ways, often illegal to shelter themselves.

Kevin W.J. McCraken (1992) while assessing 'the needs of

community services planning' said that it will provide social planners a guidance for assessing the needs of aged and disabled persons.

Margulis, H.L. (1992) highlighted the spatial restructuring of the global economy in transforming cities and altering the configuration of the global urban system. The process has required urban managers, corporate and public officials to re-examine local capacities for rationalizing land-use and promoting economic investment.

Gopalkrishnan, K.S. (1992) in his paper entitled sustainable quality of life and the metropolis describe a model for urban and environmental management that will sustain a good quality of life in urban centres.

H.S. Geyer and T.M. Kontuly (1992) analysed differential urbanization and peoples response to quality of life which may be used as peoples perceptions of their quality of life. This also points to a possible connection between differential patterns of migrations and peoples perceptions of quality of life.

Anjana P. Desai (1992) discussed about 'the Indian city: A conglomeration of culture'. She was of the opinion that the individual characteristics of cities and their style of working can be understood if one can place them within the framework of a certain cultural milieus which they belong to. The way the space is organized or the way human interactions take place depends on the shared values, specific needs, behaviour and adaptive strategies of groups of residents.

Political Aspect of Urban Life

Town Management

There is a vast difference between rural life and urban life. No doubt the basis of urban is different from rural life, but urban life has its own peculiarities and features, which have their own effect on different aspects of man's life as socially, economically, politically. Political life in the cities of Munger and Bhagalpur have their own peculiarities. Here the political life is dynamic and changes with the social needs of urban life. To meet the needs and maintain the law and order in the urban society there are two-fold aspects of political life, viz. one administrator appointed by the Government called District Magistrate; and secondly, Municipal Committee which includes the elected members as peoples representative as Mayor.

From the point of view of administration the head of the state is the Governor who commands Ministry at the state level. The state is divided into division and each division is headed by a commissioner. Each division has certain districts, which are administered by District Magistrate. The commissioner is responsible for the maintenance of law and order in the whole division, and District Magistrate is responsible for the maintenance of law and order in the district. To help the District Magistrate there is an army of officers according to the needs. There are Additional District Magistrates, City Magistrates, Divisional Magistrates, Deputy Collectors etc. Besides these officials there are tehsildars, naib tehsildars; and other officials. As the headquarter of the state, there is an Inspector General of Police on the police side, who is sided by Additional and Deputy Inspector General for division. Under his supervision there are Superintendent of Police, Deputy Superintendent of Police, in-charge of Kotwalis, Sub-Inspectors, Assistant sub-Inspectors and so on. All these people help the Government in the maintenance of law and order. In cities there are also Probationary officers who look after delinquents and juvenile criminals. There are Criminal Investigation Department also. Almost all government officials do their work in towns and cities as well.

On the other hand, there are Municipal Committees in each town there are elected representatives of people who are elected on the basis of adult franchise. These representatives are supposed to be the persons having full knowledge of the problems of their zone. But it has been seen that they fight the elections on party basis. There may be some independent members who do not have any contract with any party. These representatives are called the City Fathers and have the job of looking after the hygiene, education, water supply, electricity arrangement, medical aid, entertainment, etc. For each department, there is a committee of members. Now-a-days the Town Planning officer helps these Municipal members in ameleorating the way of urban life.

Dual Administration

From the above arrangements it would be clear that there is treble administration—one is the Central, second is the State Government and third is the local self-government by elected representatives of people. Sometimes, there is conflict between these authorities. The municipal elections are fought on party wants to have control over the Municipal Management Committee. If there is control of opposition party then the chances of conflict are more, the elections have become very costly. The candidate has to spend a lot of money. This means that he may indulge in corrupt practices after winning the election. The excessive expenditure during elections is an evil, which keeps on multiplying. Hence, the municipal chairman is not inspired by the feeling of service and do not think as he should be for the welfare of people. They become shrewd businessmen and calculate profit and loss and act accordingly. He tries to manoeuvre and manipulate to keep big contracts for his relatives and receive regular lump sum commissions from them. Along with these there is evil of casteism and groupism as well.

Thus, the urban politics has become a profession. The politics is no longer the dedication to service and welfare of people, but it has become the way of taking gain and earning money by using all sorts of notorious activities. Politics has taken the shape of business and operates strictly on the basis of profit and loss. All evil practices have guarded the modern urban politics.

But the picture of urban politics is not so gloomy as depicted above. Government officials are there at the head of the Municipal offices and there are many checks at various point by official agencies. Hence, there cannot be unfettered freedom, to practice corruption. Wherever, whenever these affairs have deteriorated the Government has right to dissolve the municipal committee. Hence, the Municipalities try to maintain their decorum and decency and try to carry out the plans put before them. The municipal chairmen have first hand knowledge of the problems of the city and, therefore, genuine and good work is carried out. A new water tank may be constructed; new road may be constructed and so on. Many times we get really dedicated people who do the real and genuine work for welfare of the people and the society.

In conclusion we may say that though the urban politics is fitted with many evils and there is influence of black money, casteism and corruption as prevalent there, but yet there is a hope of silver line in the clouds. There are some people who are inspired by the love of humanity and service to the mankind. These dedicated people do the real and genuine work and try to remove the miseries and sufferings of people.

Sources of Data

The data regarding the parameters discussed above will be procured through fieldwork with the help of questionnaire in the cities of Munger and Bhagalpur besides the published data in the district census handbook of these districts. The different caste, religion, colonies and income differentials have been collected from various sources dealing with the urban life. It includes the following :

— Level of education
— Food habit
— Artifacts
— Sociofacts
— Mentifacts
— Dress material
— Housing condition
— Occupancy rate
— Transport facilities
— Vehicles used
— Customs of marriage
— Slums and squatters.

Methods of Study

Statistical methods will be applied in the processing of data. Cartographic methods will be adopted for map-making with the help of available data. The model building, settlement and site study, study of housing conditions besides the dress material and health of people may not be ruled out.

Hypotheses Formulation

1. Life is not a bed of roses but it is related with different functionaries and hard labour.
2. Urbanism is an expression of mixed way of living and each and every work is a discrete function not related with one-another.
3. Urban life shrouds in modernity where the rule of old people, old designed buildings, and old function are considered as mode of living of bygone days.

4. Shopping, trade and industrial development are mostly the functions of people and primary activities are least important.
5. Urban life is not opposite to the rural life but they are complementary to each other, and hence, urban living is not different from rural living.
6. In urban areas, slums and squatter settlements are raising their heads but in rural areas the environment is sufficiently clear for leading a healthy life.

Geographical Personality of the Area Under Study

Munger is a city level, centre situated on the southern levee of river Ganga. Now-a-days the construction of road-*cum*-rail bridge is going on to connect Munger with Khagaria. It has been located on the latitude of 25°23' N and 86°38' E longitude. The city of Munger traces its history back from the days of *Ramayana* and *Mahabharats* upto the present. During ancient period it was a small holy place of worship especially at the time of Raja Karna when it was capital of Anga desh. At present it a district headquarter, divisional centre and centre of Imperial Tobacco Company of India. In 2001 its population was 1,87,311, and total area of 17 km^2 some of the important *mohallas* are Bari Bazar, Bekapur, Raisar, Madhopur, Mogal Bazar, Basudeopur, Laldarwaza, Chhotikelabari and Haji-Sujan. Total number of wards are 33 only (Fig. 1.2).

Bhagalpur is also a city level centre, situated on the southern levee of Ganga River. Now-a-days the construction of road bridge across the Ganga River has connected the city of Bhagalpur with Naugachhia in the north. It has been located on the latitude of 25° 15' N and longitude of 87° E. The city of Bhagalpur has old history of Champanagar of Buddhist period (Fig. 1.3).

According to 2001 census its total population was 3,40,349 covering an area of 31.17 km^2. Bhagalpur is also a district headquarter, divisional headquarter and a rare centre of silk industry in Eastern India. Some of its important *mohallas* are Nathnagar, Adampur, Ishachak, Lalbagh, Tilka-Manjhi, Bhagalpur University and important road-*cum*-railway junction of eastern Bihar. In Bhagalpur total number of wards are 37 only (Fig. 1.3).

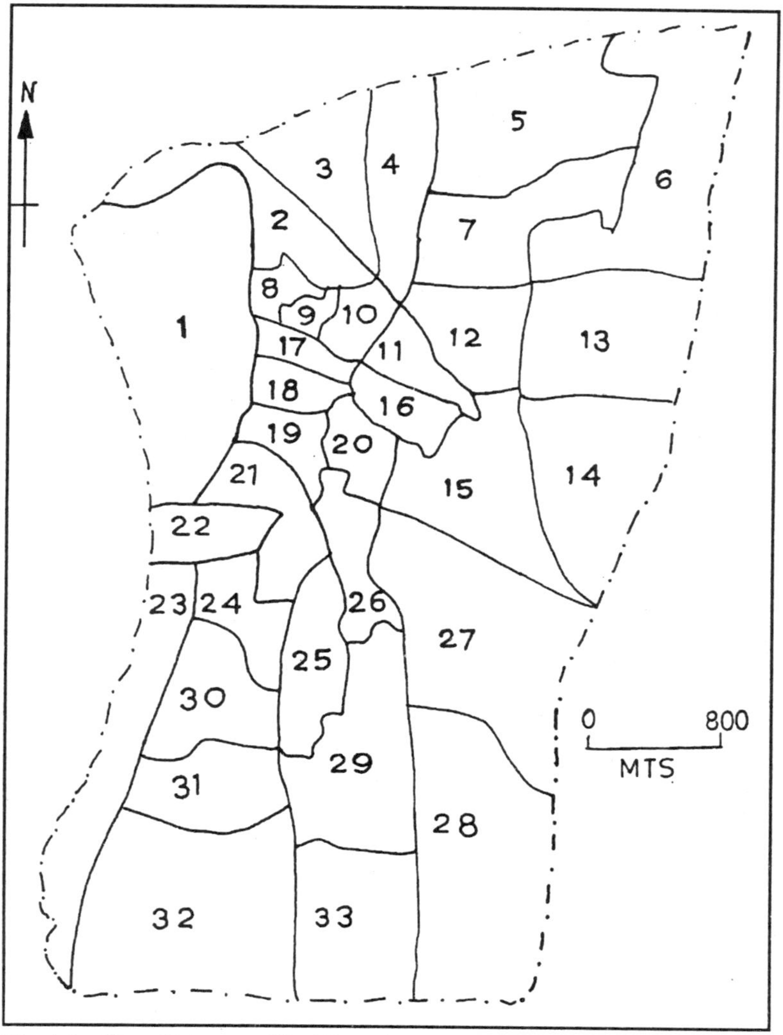

Fig. 1.2 : City of Munger : Ward Boundary

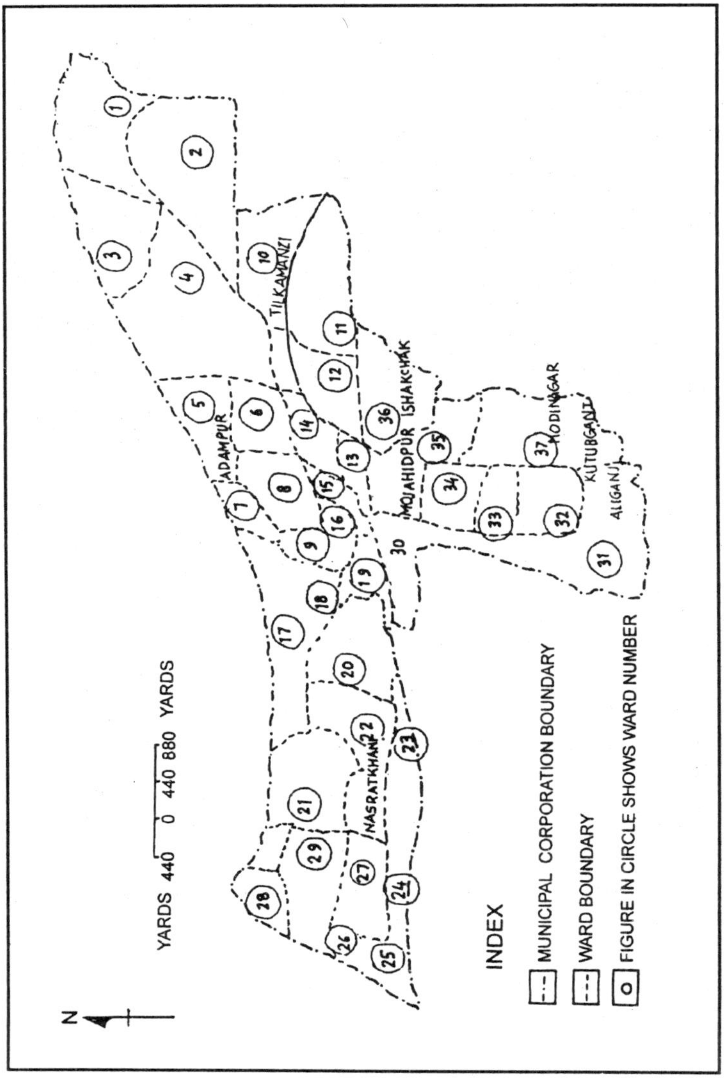

Fig 1.3 : Bhagalpur City : Ward Boundary

REFERENCES

Bhattachatya, S.N. (1999), *Rural Industrialization in India*, (Delhi, B.R. Publishing Corporation), p. 3.

"Census of India, (1991)," Series-I 1, Bihar, Provisional Population Totals, Paper 2 of 2001, p. 45.

Chelamkuri, S.V. (1999)," Population Problem in India," in *Competition Success* March 1999, Delhi, p. 55.

Cherunilam, Francis (1986), This Growing Shortage of Housing," in *Yojana*, Vol. 30, No. 18, Oct. 1-15, p. 15.

Choudhary, B.K. and Barisal, T, "Quality of Life and Development" in *Souvenir and Abstract*, National Conference on Environment, Development and Quality of Life, Organised by Department of Geography, D.D.U. Gorakhpur University Gorakhpur.

Choudhuri, B.D. Nag (1981), "The Urban Environment," in Bhargava, Gopal, *Urban Problems and Policy Perspectives*, (New Delhi, Abhinav Publications), p. 288

Dayal, p. (1968), "The Bihar Plain—A Regional Study" in *Transaction of Indian Council of Geographers,* Vol.5, Patna, p.23.

Dwivedi, P.N. (Chief editor) (2001), "Pollution: Ominous Portend," in *Yojana* Vol. 45, No. 2, p. 33.

Fakhruddin (1991) "*Quality of Urban life*," (Raipur : Rawat Publications), p. 96.

Ghosh, M. (1919) *Pataliputra :Patna*, (Patna, Law Press), pp. 3-6.

Goud, R. Sidda (1989), "Rural Electrification through Co-operatives" in *Yojana*, Vol. 33, No. 17.

Kim, T.J. (1978), "Quality of life : An Objective and Subjective Variable Analysis in Well-being" *Regional Studies*, Vol. 12, p. 409.

Knox, P. L. (1974), "Level of Living, a Conceptual Framework for Monitoring Regional Variation in Well-being" in *Regional Studies*, Vol. 8, p.1119.

Knox, P. L. (1975), *Social Well-being; A Spatial Perspective*, (Oxford), p. 31.

Lall, R. B. (1992), Urban Family as the Base of Social Stratification, p. 7.

Okamoto, K. (1992), *The Quality of Life in Metropolitan Suburbs of Japan*, IGU, New York.

Singh, B. (1992), *National Capital Region and Eco-Environmental Hazards.*

Sinha, J.N. (1961), "The Indian Working Force; Its Growth and Changing Composition," in *Census of India, Monograph*, No. 11, p. 66.

Waddel, L.A (1903), "Report on the Excavation of Pataliputra", (Calcutta).

Yadav Sheo Kumar, (1997), " Urban Environment. Problem; Issue and Challenge" in *The Social Profile: A Research Journal of Social Sciences,* Vol. 1, No. 1, p. 61.

Yadav, H. (1992), *The Rise of Slum along with the Decline and Revitalization of Cities.*

Yadav, Hiralal, "Environmental Management Plan for Urban Areas," *op.cit.*

Yadav, Sheo Kumar, (1998) "Urbanization and Quality of Life in Bihar" in Yadav, S.K. *The Social Profile- A Research Journal of Social Sciences*, Vol.2, No. 2, December 1998, p. 47.

2 ECOLOGICAL FRAMEWORK

The present study has been designed to trace out the comparative study of quality of life in the cities of Munger and Bhagalpur after considering the Geographical personalities of the study area. Generally the geographical background of a city includes the locational, physical, economic, social, demographic and functional character of the area considered for investigation. In the urban centres of Munger and Bhagalpur the quality of life revolves around the concentration of population, surrounding environment, transportation linkages, location of shopping establishments, dress material of people, food habit and the level of education and recreation of the inhabitants of the area.

Locational View

The cities of Munger and Bhagalpur are urban centres located on 25°28′ N latitude, and 86°28′ East longitude in case of Munger and 87° East longitude in case of Bhagalpur. They are the district and Divisional headquarters and considered as primate cities of the locality in terms of university level education, district and commissionary offices, high degree libraries, the location of super market and railway junctions as well. Both of them are surrounded by the river Ganga in the North and West and in case of Munger the Kali Pahari of Jamalpur Hill forms its eastern border and low lying areas of Chandan river in case of city of Bhagalpur. Both of them are situated on the southern levee of the Ganga river and have a firm site of basal rock of granite whose out crop could be seen near Kastharni Ghat in case of Munger and hard alluvium in case of the city of Bhagalpur. During ancient period the navigable Ganga provided strategic position and defensible higher site because the river was only trade route in this period. Hence, the cities of Munger and Bhagalpur are important river mart, which have earned the name of capital cities of Raja Karn and during the reign of Mir Kasim. In case of Munger Karn Choura is the highest point and in case of Bhagalpur Kuppa Ghat may be considered as highest point from where the panoramic view of the city could be observed in cardinal directions very easily. In this way, we can say that the cities of Munger and Bhaglapur have commandable strategic location and their geographic location and their geographical conditions are such that Northern plain land has been considered as grainary of Bihar could be easily seen. Southern side of these two cities are fertile lowlying area where the production of various crops are dominant where as western side is a land of intermingle of diaras, tal lands and Chaurs in the south. Northern portion of Munger and Bhagalpur are also the land of Gangetic trough, diaras and river basins. Thus it could be said that Munger and Bhagalpur are interesting and beautiful cities not only for their higher defensible site but they also provide a descent location for human settlements, transportation node, population concentration, commercial nerve centre, centre of learning and the development of industries. The cities of Munger and Bhagalpur have a long history whose references are available in *Mahabharta*, Vedas, Valmiki *Ramayana,* Ashoka's inscriptions and in several other historic investigations, viz. Huentsang's travel. Taverners travel, Buchanan's literature as well as in Rennel's map of India. The present site of fort in Munger is constructed by Mir Quasim in British Period. Karn Chaura has a copious references in *Mahabharata* (Fig. 2.1). Similarly, the ancient site of Bhagalpur could be seen in Champanagar on the north-eastern side of Nathnagar.

The central site of almost all the *mohallas* in the cities of Munger and Bhagalpur have congested housing condition and hence, they are the slums where due to congested living, dirty slums and the flow of refuge water and sewage in the side drains have deteriorated their situation beyond believable limits. In the city of Munger the important *mohallas* are Chauk Bazar, Bari Bazar, Sadipur, Bekapur, Purabsarai, Guhia Pokhar, Madhopur, Laldarwaza, Sandalpur, Lallu Pokhar and Raisar to name a few. Similarly, in the city of Bhagalpur some of the important *mohallas* are Sahebganj, Khanjarpur, Sarai, Tilakamanjhi, Lalkothi, Mundi Chak, Adampur, Patelnagar, Urdu Bazar and Champanagar (Tables 2.1, 2.1a, 2.1b, 2.1c, 2.1d).

The Regional Setting of Munger and Bhagalpur

This shows that both of them are well connected by road and rail from Jamalpur, Lakhisarai and almost all district headquarters of Bihar. The city of Bhagalpur is well connected through Vikramsila setu with

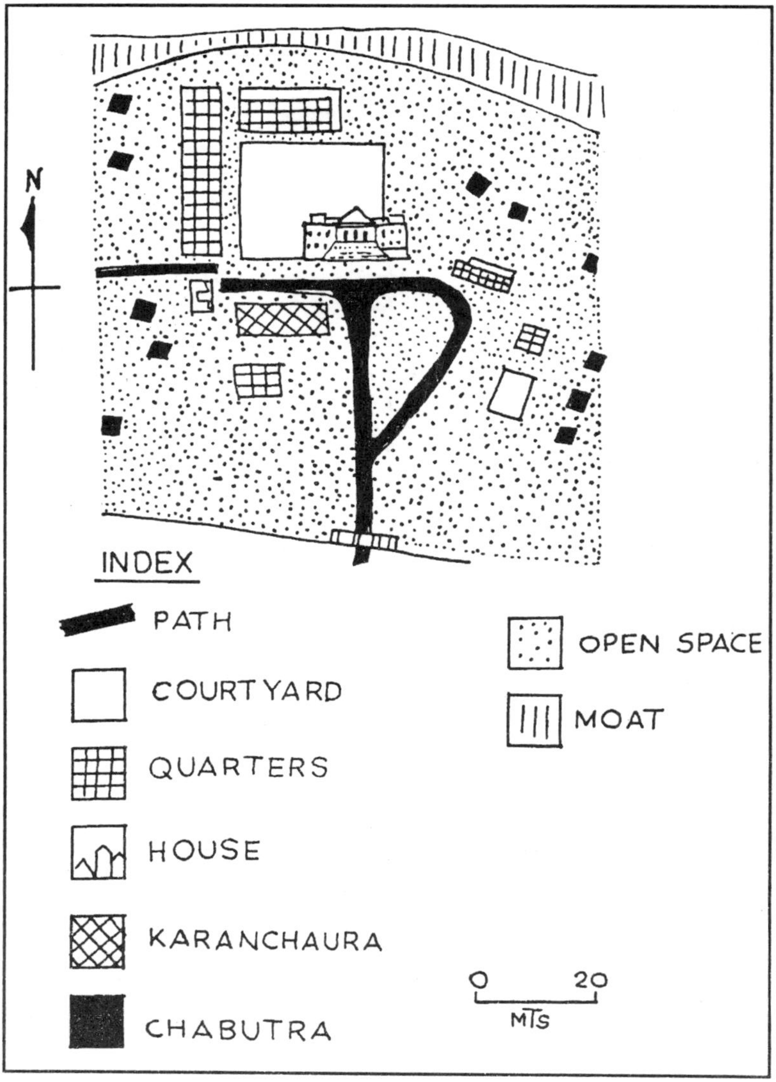

Fig. 2.1 : Karan Chaura

Naugachhia and Khagaria across the river Ganga for the present and the rail-*cum*-road bridge is under construction (Fig. 2.2).

Table 2.1 : Administrative Units of the Cities of Munger and Bhagalpur

Ward	*Munger*		*Bhagalpur*	
	Area Hectare	*Population per km² 2001*	*Area Hectare*	*Population 2001*
1.	351.56	37.80	109.89	88.21
2.	95.88	83.60	252.00	25.351
3.	92.50	105.12	226.90	48.02
4.	98.50	121.32	189.03	56.11
5.	167.19	34.87	57.74	98.99
6.	223 .14	37.29	57.74	82.14 1
7.	129.50	87.58	24.11	241.62
8.	24.06	154.03	64.39	141:47
9.	18.44	454.20	30.35	213.34
10.	28.38	217.93	124.83	80.02
11.	127.50	62.63	103.29	79.55
12.	73.75	127.99	51.64	127.60
13.	172.44	49.17	28.63	153.39
14.	189.06	21.88	38.03	170.08
15.	168.00	42.78	30.11	110.98
16.	44.38	205.42	14.74	309.41
17.	28.81	177.71	78.96	70:91
18.	26.56	241.14	39.48	128.33
19.	40.25	189.00	27.25	227.31
20.	46.56	232.40	94.06	98.73
21.	81.44	159.29	403.49	22 51
22.	48.69	96.94	116.00	62.46
23.	157.19	32.20	69.30	109.57
24.	80.06	49.47	14.85	380.29
25.	96.25	66.69	80.34	13 357
26.	52.50	150.22	10.16	633.20
27.	283.19	31.22	33.27	262.08
28.	350.25	23.78	60.60	93.30
29.	178.00	27.41	77.61	149.92
30.	108.50	68.22	58.36	80.42
31.	109.06	19.76	143 .59	61.22
32.	343.38	23.78	55.48	181.61
33.	190.50	40.68	30.74	149.46
34.	—	—	47.26	144.46
35.	—	—	155.99	49.05
36.	—	—	67.90	122.93
37.	—	—	134.05	64.04

Relief and Drainage

The city of Munger is located above 55 metres from mean sea level

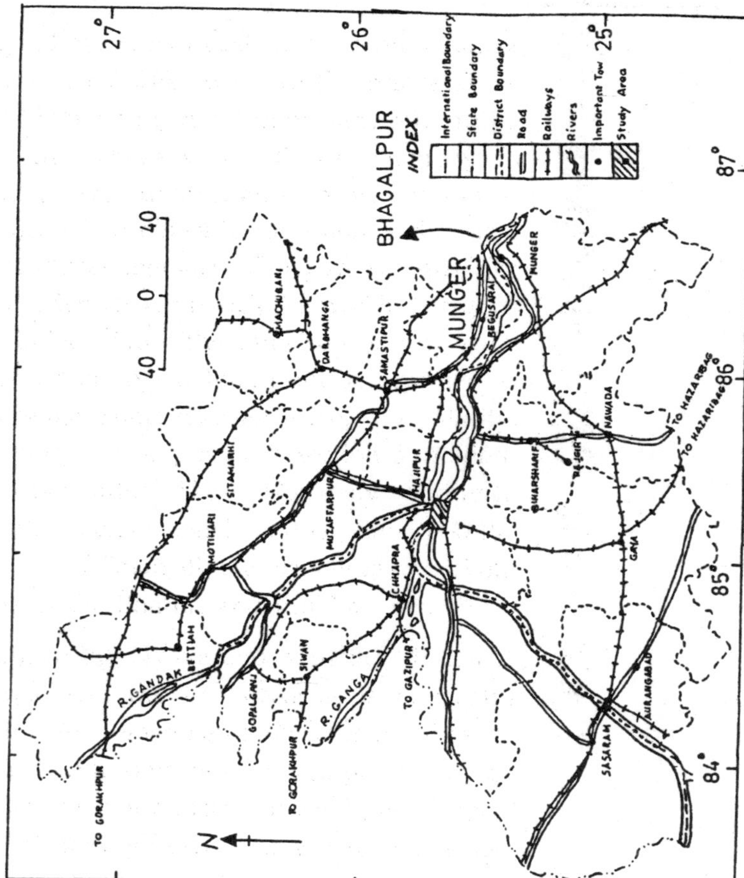

Fig. 2.2 : Cities of Munger and Bhagalpur Residential Setting

Table 2.1a : Bhagalpur City : Ward-wise Households, Sex Ratio and Total Population (2001)

Ward No.	*No. of Households*	*Population*		
		Male Population	*Female Population*	*Total*
1.	2058	6981	5888	12869
2.	1218	6169	3147	9316
3.	2093	6619	5958	12577
4.	2144	7289	6303	13592
5.	1053	3310	2828	6138
6.	1176	3366	3090	6456
7.	979	3108	2662	5770
8.	1587	5139	4459	9598
9.	936	3287	2912	6199
10.	2402	6381	7263	13644
11.	1512	523	5059	10582
12.	1807	5993	5380	11373
13.	800	2660	2315	4975
14.	1240	3955	3537	7492
15.	664	2009	1736	3805
16.	516	1813	1656	3469
17.	1600	5193	4470	9663
18.	1301	4694	4018	8712
19.	874	3340	2985	6325
20.	1852	7082	5755	12837
21.	1563	5572	4678	10250
22.	964	4089	3129	7218
23.	1205	4463	3973	8436
24.	1007	4192	3718	7910
25.	1620	6384	5695	12079
26.	818	3186	2829	6015
27.	1432	5017	4476	9493
28.	1108	3788	3323	7111
29.	1474	5915	5259	11174
30.	1832	7147	6666	13813
31.	2013	6760	5928	12688
32.	1180	4214	3731	7945
33.	1019	3842	3545	7387
34.	1577	5544	4823	10367
35.	1687	5786	5147	10933
36.	1819	5962	5224	11186
37.	1941	6092	5278	11370

and the city of Bhagalpur has a height of 45 metres. In Munger, the highest point is Karn Chaura whose height of 125 metre from mean sea level and city of Bhagalpur the heighest point is Mirjan at in the south. The lowest point in the city of Munger is Mirchia Tank besides

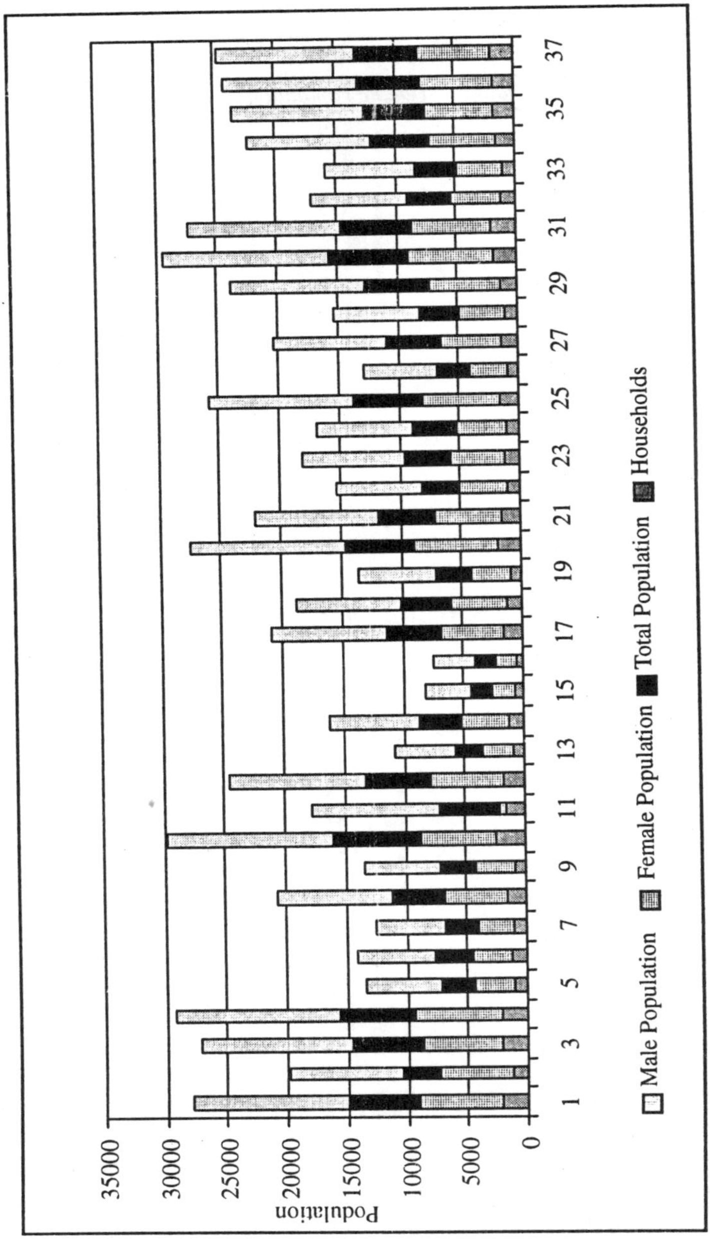

Graph 2.1 : Bhagalpur City : Ward-wise Households, Sex Ratio and Total Population (2001)

Table 2.1b : Bhagalpur City : Ward-wise Scheduled Caste Total Population (2001)

Ward No.	*Population*		
	Male Population	*Female Population*	*Total*
1.	723	558	1281
2.	653	422	1075
3.	854	753	1607
4.	650	539	1189
5.	159	131	290
6.	144	131	275
7.	358	322	680
8.	427	386	813
9.	221	181	402
10.	807	728	1535
11.	9	11	20
12.	553	500	103
13.	38	30	68
14.	450	399	849
15.	90	88	178
16.	0	0	0
17.	286	249	535
18.	459	417	876
19.	93	90	183
20.	833	489	1322
21.	239	221	460
22.	330	220	550
23.	667	589	126
24.	52	47	99
25.	47	40	87
26.	88	74	162
27.	523	468	991
28.	102	81	183
29.	347	289	476
30.	111	107	218
31.	157	1073	2230
32.	240	236	476
33.	201	202	403
34.	564	520	1084
35.	513	439	952
36.	451	422	873
37.	828	754	1582

Raja Tank and Rani Tank in the Fort area along with the Kastaharani Ghat on the bank Ganga. The lowest point in the city of Bhaglapur is Golaghat on the embankment of the Ganga river. So far as the general condition is concerned in Munger, Basudeopur, Madhopur and Mogal Bazar are the *mohallas* of high relief feature but in the city of Bhagalpur

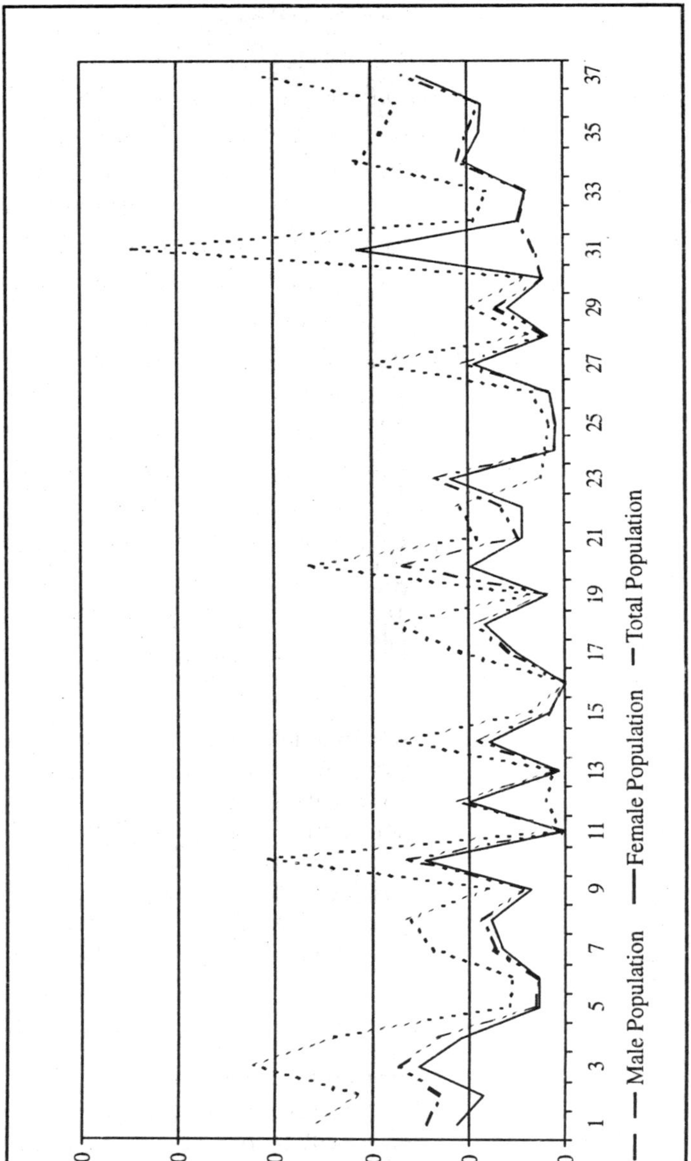

Graph 2.2 : Bhagalpur City : Ward-wise Scheduled Caste Population (2001)

Table 2.1c : Bhagalpur City : Ward-wise Scheduled Tribe Total Population (2001)

Ward No.	*Population*		
	Male Population	*Female Population*	*Total*
1.	2	7	9
2.	371	39	410
3.	40	161	201
4.	35	31	66
5.	8	6	14
6.	33	47	80
7.	0	0	0
8.	2	0	2
9.	6	9	15
10.	29	25	54
11.	10	3	13
12.	2	0	2
13.	7	7	14
14.	58	55	113
15.	0	0	0
16.	3	3	6
17.	3	2	5
18.	9	3	12
19.	0	0	0
20.	28	21	49
21.	98	58	156
22.	53	9	62
23.	0	0	0
24.	0	0	0
25.	0	0	0
26.	0	0	0
27.	2	2	4
28.	0	0	0
29.	43	25	68
30.	5	1	6
31.	120	103	223
32.	3	1	4
33.	0	0	0
34.	0	0	0
35.	10	6	16
36.	10	8	18
37.	3	2	5

the entire southern portion south of railway line is the highest area from where the slope of land is towards the Ganga river in the north. The drainage lines of these two cities are draining the dirty water as well as the water received from natural rain towards the Ganga river

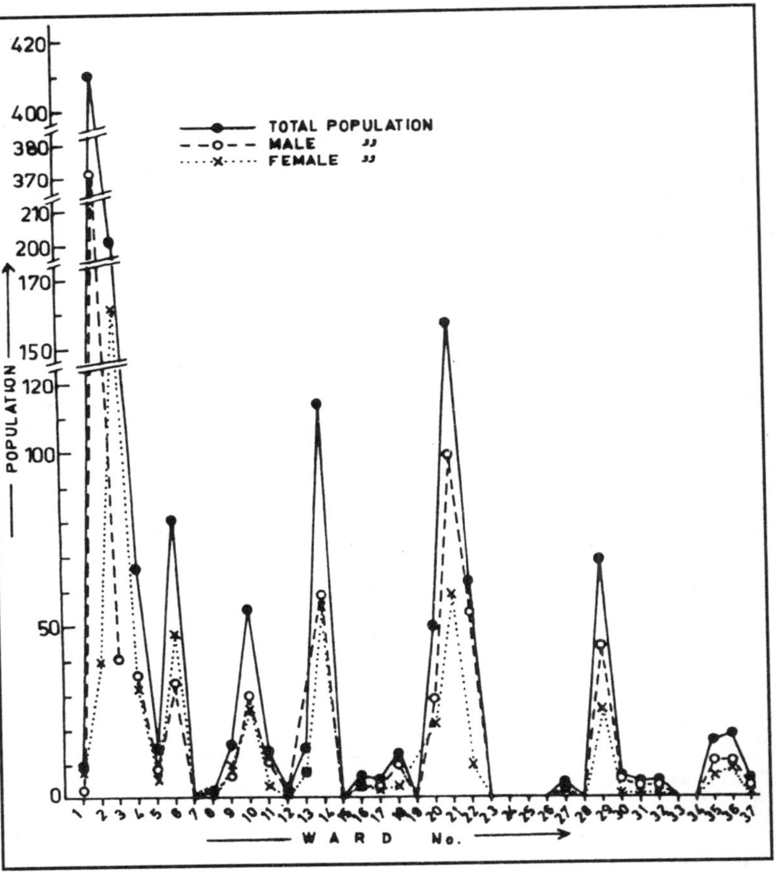

Graph 2.3 : Bhagalpur City Ward-wise Scheduled Tribe Population (2001)

Table 2.1d : Bhagalpur City Ward-wise Identifed Slum Area and Slum Dwellers

S.No.	*Ward No.*	*Name of Slum Area*	*Population of SC*
1.	31	Jarlaha Mehtar Toli	4698
2.	30	Maulana Chack Pashushala	4697
3.	34	Hasan Ganj, Dom Toli	5784
4.	33	Hussainabad	5784
5.	35	Sikandarpur, Harijan Tola	7474
6.	32	Maheshpur Harijan Tola	9236
7.	13	Ramser Mehtar Tola	4500
8.	17	Jogsar Mehtar Tola	4931
9.	20	Bari Khanjarpur, Dom Tola	4609
10.	21	Bari Khanjarpur, Mushar Tola	4500
11.	23	Barari Mushar Tola	2225
12.	18	Maya Mushar Tola	2609
13.	24	Sacchidanand Nagar	3643
14.	2	Mayaganj Sunder Wan	631
15.	5	Nathnagar Kundia Tola	4625
16.	7	Garhkachari, Champanagar	1662
17.	1	Lalu Chack and Bhudhu Chack	2464
18.	4	Baisbhighi Mohalla, Champanagar	2679
19.	13	Urdu Bazar, Wajid Lane	7697
20.	26	Bhojanpur, Harijan Tola	13323
21.	37	Nayachack, Harijan Tola	4946
22.	28	Mundi Chack, Mehtar Tola	6562
23.	38	Kutubganj, Harijan Tola	5314
24.	24	Jawaharpur, Mehtar Tola	3884
25.	18	Choti Khanjarpur	3880

in the north. In the central northern part several residential *mohallas* are located but unfortunately due to congestion of houses and high density of population most of them have developed as slum areas such as Adampur. Ishakchak, Tatarpur, Parwatti in the city of Bhagalpur and Guhia Pokhar, Topkhan Bazar, Raisar Murgiachak and Mogal Bazar in the city of Munger. All these have posed deteriorating situation regarding the quality of life of people in these two cities (Fig. 2.3).

Climatic Conditions

The cities of Munger and Bhagalpur are located in sub-tropical monsoon climate where the general climate is not as wet as West Bengal and the dryness is as found in western part of Saran and Bhojpur. The mean monthly temperature is 18°C. The mean daily

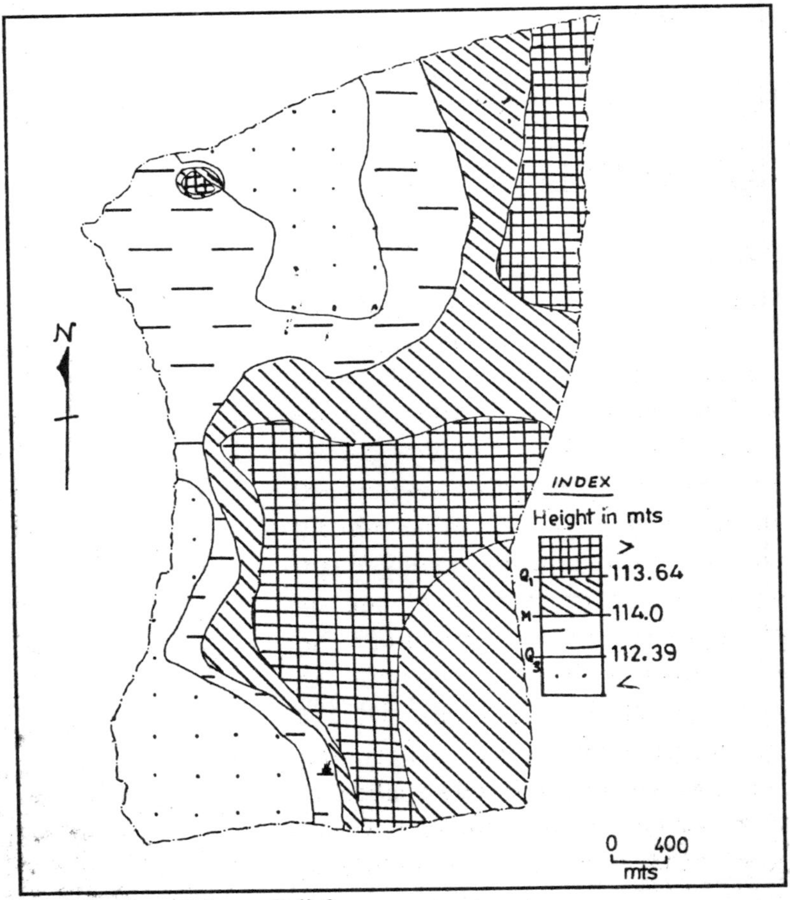

Fig. 2.3 : City of Munger Relief

maximum temperature is 38°C in the month of May and the mean lowest temperature is 11°C in January (Fig. 2.4).

So far as rainfall is concerned monsoon usually breaks in the third week of June and continues till September and October. Although the temperature falls down but the heat is oppressive especially in the day while it is stuffy and sultry during the night. The average rainfall being 19cm, 33cm, 29cm and 24cm in June, July, August and September respectively.

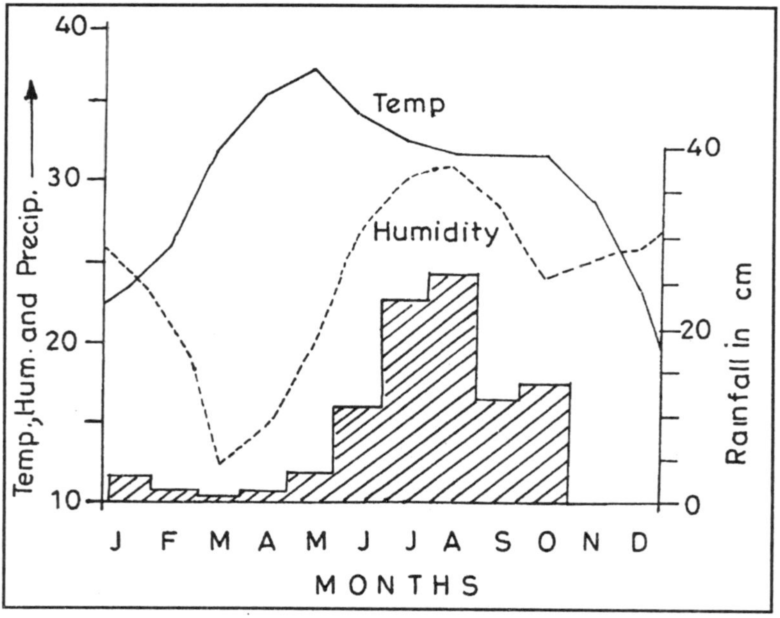

Fig. 2.4 : City of Munger Temperature, Humidity and Precipitalion Graph (2004)

In the cities of Munger and Bhagalpur the cold season starts in November and lingers up to February. In November the morning and evening are cool while in December and January due to sudden cooling of atmosphere the night is very cold. March is progressively warmer until the hot weather sets in the middle of March. Fig. 2.4 shows the distribution of temperature, humidity and rainfall of the city of Munger. Although the highest temperature goes upto 45° occasionally in May but the lowest temperature is just 11°C in January. In summer months of May and June the local heat wave "*Loo*" is quite prevalent in the cities of Munger and Bhagalpur.

The relative humidity is about 75 per cent in July and September to about 90 per cent in August but it is as low as 50 per cent in the month of May. The surrounding areas of the cities of Munger and Bhagalpur present mosquito breeding ground on stagnant dirty water which quite often give rise to Malaria, Influenza and Kalazar epidemics in these two cities.

So far as the cities climate is concerned the minor variations could be observed specially during winter nights when the market area of the cities are relatively warmer in comparison with fringe area of these cities. Even in day time due to generators, metalled road, tall building and high concentration of population, the central markets remain more warmer in comparison with sub-urban area.

Soils and Vegetation

In southern portion of the cities of Munger and Bhagalpur reddish alluvium soil for older alluvium is found which has been deposited by the floodwater of the Ganga river and others. In the central part of these cities light red with sufficient adhesive capacity soil is found which provide a firm base for human habitations and favourable site for the preparation of titles or bricks. For the fact, most of the chimney's of the cities of Munger and Bhagalpur are located in north western part of Lallupokhar and west of Nathnagar and north eastern part of Chandi Asthan, Bararighat etc. Near the embankment of the river sandy soil is found both in the cities of Munger and Bhagalpur due to annual flooding along the Ganga river.

So far as the vegetation is concerned the cities of Munger and Bhagalpur has deciduous forest cover. Natural vegetation is found in localities near rivers, ditches and pynes etc. Almost all-fencing system as hedge around the houses is done by planting small trees and flowery plants. Vegetation zone is known as green spot of the city from Bank village in the east upto Safiasarai in the South and riverine vegetation of the Ganga in the north upto the riverine vegetation of fort, and Lallupokhar in the West. All the marginal areas of railways and human settlement, the land is covered with bushy vegetation. The situation is more or less same in the city of Bhagalpur as well. The main species of plants are Behaya, Sinuar, Sheo Babul, Mirchaiya, Kataiya etc. which never provide healthy climate for human living because most of the city dwellers use the same for fuel and the area may be considered as vast latrine ground in the heart of these two cities. The green spots are also areas of the dumps of garbage, extraction of soil, vice of under worlds, e.g. murder, stealing and making the life of city dwellers insecure by robbers and thieves specially during night hours. At places Mango, Sesam, Guava, Palm, Deit, Semal, Mahua and Plantain are seen in a haphazard manner, which are breaking the monotony of urban life and humdrum reality of the urban area. Green spots cover about 50 hectares of land in the city of Munger and

75 hectares of land in the city of Bhagalpur. This encompasses both natural and planted vegetation cover.

Functional Zones of the Cities

Function's are of the types :

(a) Primary function,
(b) Secondary function,
(c) Tertiary function,
(d) Quarternary function, and
(e) Quinary function.

In the cities of Munger and Bhagalpur almost all these functions are carry on by the inhabitants either for promoting his business or getting a job in the field, factories, shops, schools, colleges and Government offices. All these functions which have a direct relation with crops, vegetables, minerals and wood cutting are taken as primary function in the cities of Munger and Bhagalpur. Market gardening, raising of food crops, cutting of forest, digging of soil from the land all are primary functions where as cigarette factory, gun factory, saw milling, Printing Press, flour mill all are known as secondary function in which the conversion of primary goods into secondary is done with the process of manufacturing, e.g. wood cutting is primary function, chair making is a secondary function, selling of chair is a tertiary function, giving the knowledge of chair making by direct contact is a quarternary function and the direction by the superior about chair making or wood cutting or chair selling is a quinary function.

Due to wider extent of Bhagalpur city the quality of life is more complex and the industrial goods are cheaper in comparison with the city of Munger. But the agricultural products are relatively cheaper in Munger in comparison with Bhagalpur.

In the cities of Munger and Bhagalpur almost all functions of the city level centres are available. These functions are performed haphazardly in different parts of the city (Fig. 2.5.). Table 2.2 shows the area of different functional zones in the cities of Munger and Bhagalpur.

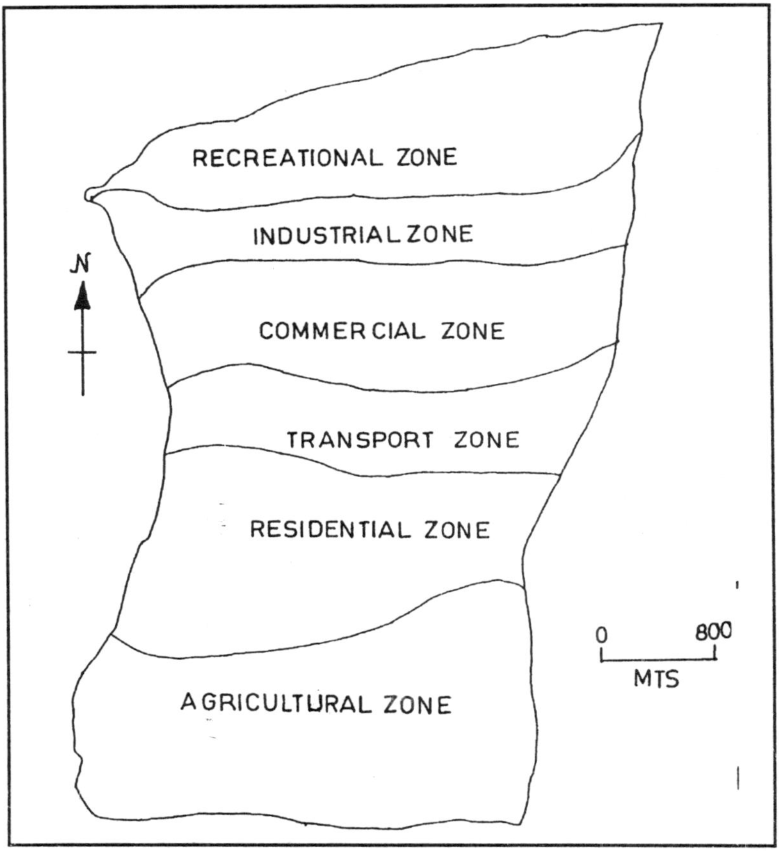

Fig. 2.5 : Munger Functional Zone

Transport Zone

Munger has an awkward location with special reference to the transport routes because Munger lies far-off from the tract of Kiul-Bhagalpur loop line. Therefore, Munger-Jamalpur rail line only acts as sub-urban railway. Inside the city Purabsarai and Munger Junctions are located besides bus depot in Shastri Nagar and bus stand near town hall. Fort and Purabsarai are some of the important transport nodes of the city which act as the nerve centers because they provide life line to the city.

Table 2.2 : Functional Zones of the Cities of Munger and Bhagalpur

Sl. No.	*Zones*	*Area in Munger Sq. Metre '000*	*Area in Bhagalpur in Hectare*
1.	Residential	9673	5560
2.	Commercial	760	705
3.	Industrial	167	750
4.	Institutional	250	1861
5	Educational	124	1189
6.	Community Services	1694	189
7.	Public utilities	1000	1153
8.	Transport	113	3216
	Open Space	3728	4916
	Total	17,500	18,352

Source : Calculated from ward Map.

In the city of Bhagalpur there is an aerodrum at Jawaripur near Tilka Manjhi. There are three railway stations, e.g. Nathnagar, Bhagalpur Junction and Sabour. The bus stands are located at Aliganj, Tilaka Manjhi and the other just near railway junction. The entire city is well connected with metalled road. The tempos are running from railway station to zero mile and Champanagar to Mandroja.

Commercial Zone

Commercial zone of Munger city is located in such a fashion that it resembles the shape of a bird sitting in the center of the city map (Fig. 2.6). This forms the central business district which comprises the area from Chauk Bazar, Kara Maidan (Gola), Munger Ghat, Chuabagh, Sandalpur, Laldarwaza, etc. This zone is not expanding due to higher price of land in the city centre and the barriers of the residential areas. In recent decade due to the separation of Begusarai district from Munger it has highly affected the consumers activity of the city. Similarly, the creation of Lakhisarai Sub-division and the separation of S.D.O court have highly affected the consumer behaviour of the city. There are about 4000 shops in this zone from the business centre of the city. This zone comprises the *mohallas* of Nimtalla, Fort area, Sharwan bazaar, Chuabagh, Laldarwaza, Chotikelawari, Purabsarai, Kaura Maidan, Guhea Pokhar, Chauk area and Sadipur of the city besides Safiabad as outlying node.

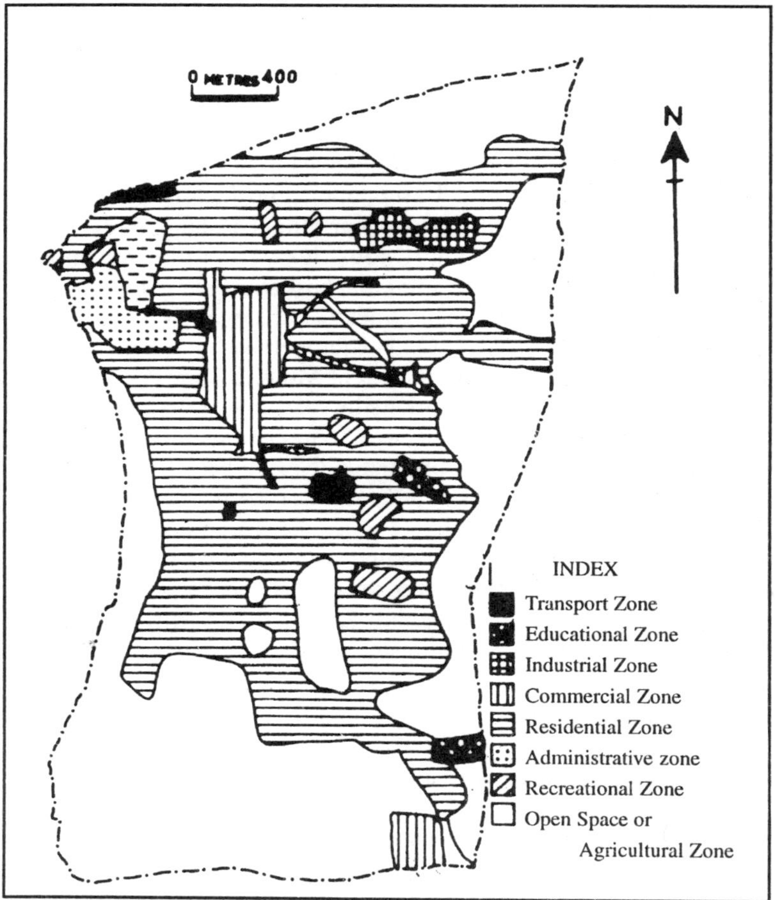

Fig. 2.6 : Functional Zones of the City of Munger

In the city of Bhagalpur the commercial zone runs from Nathnagar in the west upto Jawaripur in the east a distance of about 7 kilometres and from Aliganj in the south upto the Ganga bridge in the north. In the central part some of the important commercial centres are Guradwara road, Khalifabag chowk, station road, Parwatti and Tilka Manjhi chowk. The goods sold in these market are mostly clothes, utensils, medicines, shoes, cycle stores, readymade garments and electrical goods. The market centres open at 9 a.m. in the morning and close at 9 p.m. in the evening. The buyers mostly come from different residential areas of the city along with the surrounding zone of influence.

Industrial Zone

The industrial zone of the city of Munger is found in detached location such as cigarette factory of Basudeopur, gun factory of fort area, thresher making and grill factory near Nilam Road, Chauk Bazar, Bekapur, Nimtalla, etc. Other industries of the city are mostly household, biri making, hand spinning, basket weaving, oil crushing, medicine and saline water making near Khankah and other places.

The cigarette factory (I.T.C.) is equipped with modern technical machinery helped in the development of Munger from 1921 up to the present. There loere 25,000 workers in 1980.

According to Table 2.3 there are 616 industrial units in the city of Bhagalpur which have been distributed over 39 hectares of area and the total number of workers employed are 23,448 only. There are altogether 21 industrial units of rice, oil, flour concentrated in Merjanhat area. The city of Bhagalpur is reputed centre for silk and handloom clothes. The important centres are Nathnagar, Champanagar, Khanjarpur, Lodipur, Hussainabad, Kabirpur and Mirjanhat areas. These are several household industries in the city of Bhagalpur.

Administrative Zone

It includes the district court, sub-divisional court, municipal office,

Table 2.3 : Industrial Status of the Bhagalpur City, 2004

Sl. No.	*Industry*	*No. of Units*	*Area in Hectare*	*Persons Employed*
1.	Food Products	21	11	16
2.	Silk and Handloom	221	10	22,000
3.	Printing Press	21	2	105
4.	Chemical	64	5	192
5.	Saw Mills and Furniture	17	2	55
6.	Metal Products	50	5	250
7.	Shoe Making	10	1	25
8.	Biri Making	22	3	615
	Total	616	39	23,448

Source : District Industry Office, Bhagalpur.

Police station and other offices of the government located specially in Fort area, Raja Bazar, Purabsarai Fanri besides a lot of government offices located in different parts of the city in a haphazard way. Police line is located at Hathiagarh and Laldarwaza with a vast parade ground.

In the city of Bhagalpur the administrative zone is located in the court premises at Adampur. At this place commissioners office, district and sub-divisional courts are located along with consumer's forum, income tax office and chamber of commerce as well Post office, Telephone office, electricity office and others are located in different parts of the city.

Educational Zone

Educational zone of the city is very small where R.D. and D.J. College, J.R.S. College, J.M.S. College, B.R.M. College, Science College, besides Teachers Training School in Purabsarai, Zila school at Topkhana Bazar, Model school at Bari Bazar, City school at Ghosi tola, Training school at Belan Bazar, Durga Santha School at Sahzubair Road, Urdu School at Chauramba, Nand Kumar High School at Basudeopur, Madhopur Girls School at Madhopur, Notredam, Upendra Training and Baijnath Girls School at Piparpanti Road are some of the important centres of learning found in Munger. There are several other schools in the city whose number is as follows: Recognized shorthand typewriting and other vocational training institute, Higher Secondary or Secondary School-10, Junior Secondary/Middle School - 28, Primary School - 76 and Public Library including reading room- 2.

In the Bhagalpur city the zone of education comes under the premises of Tilka Manjhi Bhagalpur University. Some of the important college, e.g. T.N.B. College, Marwari College, B.N. College, different P.G. Departments, computer centre and sericulture colleges are found. S.M. College is located in Khanjarpur *mohalla* of the city. Besides these, there are 35 High English Schools, 45 Middle Schools and 125 Primary Schools and Makhtab are found in different localities of the city.

Religious Centres

Munger is well known for its religious centres specially in North Bihar. At Kastharni Ghat lakhs of people take holy bath in the Ganga who came after travelling from thousands of kilometres in rural areas. Other religious centres are Chandiasthan, Bihar School of Yoga, Mahabir Asthan, Shivalayas, Khankah Mazar of Pir Nafa Saheb, besides Bari Durga Asthan and several other temples of Lord Shiva, Hanumanji and Mosques which are found in several parts of the city.

Open Space and Agricultural Field

Open space and agricultural fields are found in the Munger city at several places such as at Sandalpur, Guhea Pokhar, Laldarwaza, Sadipur, Hemjapur and Bari Bazar having agricultural field of paddy, wheat and vegetables. The railway track has open space especially north of Purabsarai railway station.

Water and Electric Supply

Water Supply

The city of Munger gets *drinking* water from Kasturba Water Works of Munger Municipality with headquarter in Bari Bazar. It has a daily capacity of supplying 10.46 million gallons of water to different parts of the city. The water tanks are found at Kasturba Water Works, Guhea Pokhar, Hospital, Fort and Hathiagarh. Almost all important residential areas of the city are served with Municipal Water Supply.

Electricity Supply

The city of Munger receives electric supply from Barauni Thermal Power, D.V.C. and Patratu. Primarily it has been designed to get electricity from Barauni Thermal Power Project but in case of emergency D.V.C. and Patratu also supply. In the city of Munger 5,474 connections have been given to houses of different consumers, 234 to industrial houses, 1,917 to commercial establishments, 1,431 to bulb points on roads and others include 397 connections in government offices and educational institutions.

Residential Zone

Residential function occupies the greater Chunk of the city Surface e.g. more than 50 per cent has been occupied by residential quarters in different *mohallas* in Madhopur, Raisar, Sadipur, Ghositola, Kaura Maidan, Dilawarpur, Topkhana Bazar, Mogal bazaar, Basudeopur and others. Even in residential areas the condition of living is very haphazard because different people of different castes live together and no functional or caste homogeneity is observed because almost all people are immigrants to the city who came from rural areas either permanently or temporarily to work in industries, government offices, transport lines, educational institutions besides trade and commerce. In residential areas besides caste heterogeneity the dissimilar nature of building and haphazard location of houses are the rule in urban areas.

Recreational Zone

This zone of the city of Munger is poorly adjusted where only three cinema halls like Neelam Talkies, Vijay Talkies, Baidyanath Talkies and Zoo at Company Bagh, Pologround as play field, R.D. and D.J. College Playground besides Munger Lions Club, Cigarette factory club and Patel clubs are functioning.

Besides these there is one fire fighting brigade at Kasturba water works, Bari Bazar. There are 920 water borne latrines, 7,536 service latrines and others are found in the city which show that the environmental pollution is more acute. The Municipality should immediately try to convert the same in sanitary latrines into water borne one as it is necessary to make healthy environment of the city. Night soil is disposed of through head load septic tank latrine method in the city. In sewerage system *Pucca* Nala, *Kutcha* Nala and open drains are prevalent.

REFERENCES

Cunningham, A. (1871), *Ancient Geography of India,* p. 476.

Declaration of the Vancouver Symposium on Human Habitat, Ecology, *Quarterly Information Bulletin*, The Indian Ecological Society, Ludhiana, Vol.1. June 1977, No.2. J.R. Etherington; *Environment and Plat Ecology*, Wiley Eastern Limited, New Delhi, 1975.

Hommer, C. and Rogoff, N. (1966), "Relative Merits of Various Formulas for Rates of Growth," Unpublished Monograph, Columbia University, Quoted by J. P. Gibbs, Urban Research Method, New Delhi, p. 107.

Isard, W., (1975), "Methods of Regional Analysis". An Introduction to Regional Science, New York, 1960, Chapter II and Indian Geographical Studies, R.B. No. 5, p. 22.

Mandal, R.B. (1972), "The Geography of Rural Settlements in Bihar Plain," Unpublished Ph.D. Thesis, Patna University.

Prasad, S.D. (1964), " Census of India," 1961, District Census Handbook, Munger, Bihar Government Press, Patna.

Ram, L.N. (1969), "Impact of Population Growth on Land in Bihar," *Essays in Geography* (Ed. K.N. Das), Bhagalpur, p.130.

Roy Choudhary, P.C. (1960), *Bihar District Gazetteer*, Munger, Secretariat Press, Bihar, Patna, p. 541.

Singh, R.R.P. (1978), "*Karanchaura: Ateet Aur Vartman*" (in Hindi), Bihar School of Yoga.

Sinha, P. (1973), "Urban Functions : A Case Study of Muzaffarpur," *Indian Geographical Bulletin* R.B. No. 1, September, p. 1.

3 FACTORS AFFECTING URBAN LIFE

The factors affecting urban life in the urban centres of Munger and Bhagalpur are both physical and cultural in nature. Among the physical factors the terrain conditions on which the cities have been sited. The climatic and atmospheric conditions, which change according to seasonal vicissitudes, types of vegetation and crops grown in the area, differences in the regime of the Ganga river along with the wild animals found in the area.

Among the man-made factors the infrastructure facilities of roads, railways, number of persons per residential house, art, theatre, cinema houses, schools, college, training institutes, water supply, sanitation, provision of garbage disposal, administrative peace, facilities of sports, games and the quality of food available to the people counts much (Table 3.1).

Quality of Water Supply

The supply of safe drinking water is needed for almost all the people. But the water supply in urban area of Munger and Bhagalpur is inadequate and full of dirts and dusts. The drinking of unfiltered water is always risky because that may cause roundworm, hookworm, jaundice and several other forms of diseases.

Occupancy Rate

In the urban centre of Munger and Bhagalpur the occupancy rate varies from 4 persons per room to 8 persons per room. Occupancy rate is a sign of level of overcrowding of population in a particular family. In the cities of Munger and Bhagalpur more than 6 persons reside in one room.

Terrain Condition

The mode of terrain is decided by the ups and downs of land in the

Table 3.1 : Factors Affecting Urban Life

There are several factors which affect Urban life in the cities of Munger and Bhagalpur. The delineation of some of these factors will find place in this Project report.

Factor Affecting Quality of Life

- Residential Problem
- Caste Factor
- Levels of Theft and Burglery
- Quality of Water Supply
- Occupancy Rate
- Terrain Condition
- Atmospheric Condition
- Sanitation
- Types of Vegetation and Crops
- Caste Differentiation
- Educational Level
- Income Differentiation
- Industrial Scenario
- Rise of Slum
- Festivals in the City
- Housing Designs and Quality
- Religious Performance
- Dress Materials of People
- Food Habit of Residents
- Dance, Music, Art and Science of People
- Flood Problem
- Crime Rate
- Standard of Living
- Provision of Recreation
- Standard of Shopping Centres
- Administrative Peace
- Alcoholism
- Difficulties in Urban Travelling

city. Generally, well of people resides in upland area where as poors reside on fringe of the city especially in lowlying area where the price of the land is relatively less. Terrain is the guiding factor of flow of water either through drains or surface run-off of rainwater.

Atmospheric Condition

For the development of a city, market centre, and commercial centre the availability of salubrious climate is quite essential. The temperature around 30°C, the rainfall amounting to 150 cm annually, lack of gales, etc. are essential. Dry climate, heavy downpour and snowfall are not conducive for a good marketing environment.

Sanitation

Better sanitation is pre-requisite for the growth and development of a city. Cleanliness of the city, lighting arrangement, dump of garbage at requisite place and proper planning of the municipal localities are quite essential for a sanitary environment.

Types of Vegetation and Crops

Normal growth of vegetation and agriculturally productive hinterland have been considered essential for the proper growth of a city. Forest environment repel urban development and so is the excessive importance of crop production. So far as the cities of Munger and Bhagalpur are concerned it is neither forested nor too poor in crop production.

Caste Differentiation

Caste differentiations still found in the Hindu society. The whole society is divided into religion and castes. Hindu, Muslim, Christian, Sikh, Parsi are the main religious segments while Rajput, Brahmin, Kurmi and Yadav, are the dominant castes found in the urban life of Munger and Bhagalpur.

The Level of Education

The number of literate persons in a society decides the level of education. This could also be done with the presence of schools and colleges in an urban centres. Munger and Bhagalpur are on the threshold of educational development. They have old history of urban and educational development due to its involvement in war in the annals of the growth and development of Anga Plain.

Income Differentiation

The society could also be divided into different groups on the basis of income, i.e. high income group; medium income group and low income group. The urban life of these people also varies considerably. The living standard of rich people are always better while the poor people living in slums and squatter settlements have deplorable condition.

Industrial Scenario

In the urban centres of Munger and Bhagalpur the light industries like bakery, oil ghani, flour mill, saw mill and rice mills are found in different localities. All these provide employment to the people, but they create nuisance in the residential area along with polluting the environment. Industry has the capacity to provide sustenance to more and more people but it is not easy to manage the affairs of the industry without proper open space and arrangement of sufficient amount of capital.

Rise of Slums

In Munger and Bhagalpur slums have cropped up at several localities due to service latrine, congested living, conversion of old villages into urban fold along with the poor maintenance of garbage disposal, open drains and excessive use of generators and refrigerators which release obnoxious gases in the environment. Poverty of people is the main cause of all these evils.

Festivities in the City

The urban life of Munger and Bhagalpur is full of festivals, e.g. Durga Puja in October, the festival of colour, i.e. Holi in March, Chhath the Sun worship in November, Saraswati Puja on the eve of Basant

Panchmi in February, Kartik Purnima bath and Maghi Purnima bath in the holy Ganga river, Tila Sankranti on 14th of January along with Christmas day on 25th of December and Ganesh Puja in September are important. Besides these, several other festive occasions come such as Deepawali the festival of light, Anant Puja, worship of house deity in Ghari and Ganga Deshara in the month of June. The cultural variations and life of urbanites in the cities of Munger and Bhagalpur could be seen as colourful and joyable occasions.

Housing Designs

The designs of houses also help in the differentiation of quality of life. Multi-storey building, tile roofed houses, tin scan houses of refugees along with poor men's hutments are quite different from one another. The house types of Hindus are relatively more open in comparison with houses of the Muslims. This happens because Muslim believes more and more in *Purdah* system.

Religious Performance

From the religious point of view Hindus believe more in worship of idols, whereas Muslims read *Namaj* in mosques, Christians do prayer of Jesus Christ in the Church and Sikh people do prayer to Guru Nanak in Gurdwaras. Besides these, Hindus keep themselves without taking food on religious occasions, Muslims keep themselves hungry at the time of Ramjan and this practice is not found among Christians. Religious performance has been considered as pious act in almost all religion.

Dress Material of People

The people of Munger and Bhagalpur cities are ready to wear any kind of dress because they perceive the innovation earlier unlike other cities. They always perceive the developed fashions of the society. This makes strong base of urban life. The young urbanites are becoming more fashion conscious and they are better exposed to quick change. Munger and Bhagalpur urban area provides a complete family fashion store with something for everyone. So the urban streets are found shops full of bags, belts, shoes, costumes, jewellery, perfume and even laces of the shoes. Hence, in the cities of Munger and

Bhagalpur specialized shops of cap, sports, toys, lady's wear and gent's wear are found.

Food Habit of Residents

In urban area those people who are well off they take much better balanced food in comparison with poor people. Among the urbanites the bread, cake, jelly, cream, ice cream, soup and the amount of meat, fish and eggs are relatively higher in percentage in comparison with rural people. On the whole, urbanites prefer ready-made food but not the rural people.

Dance, Music, Art and Science

Urbanites like dance, music and art more than rural folk. Among them art painting is more popular. Music and dance come under fine arts. Among art Ramlila is more liked by the people of Munger and Bhagalpur. Under the category of science the use of telephone, computer, training of radio mechanic, motor mechanic, motorcycle and television repairing are more important. The learning of dance and music are common practice among the school going and college girls.

Problems of Flood

Due to the nearness of Ganga river flood is a rampant problem especially during the rainy season on the northern fringe of Munger and Bhagalpur urban centres. Flood was observed especially in 1954,1987, 1992, 2001 and 2003 as well. The problem is acute especially for the poors and vegetable growers around the market centre as knee deep to neck deep water flows in Lalbag, Sahebganj, Champanagar and Barari of Bhagalpur and in Laldarwaja, Chandi Asthan and Chuabag of Munger.

Crime Rate

In the urban areas of Munger and Bhagalpur the refinement of crime could be seen in terms of the use of gun, revolver, and attack with bomb, use of land mines by the rival gang of criminals at several occasions. Now-a-days, food poisoning, suicide, dacoity and theft are common practices and what to talk of murder of public as even the police personnel's feel themselves unsafe. Use of unfair means in the examination, rape, kidnapping, murder and atrocities on Harijans are rampant everywhere.

Standard of Living

In Indian cities like Munger and Bhagalpur the standard of living is very low. Income of the public is so low that they cannot afford full meal of balanced food and what to talk of nutritious food. Anyhow the general public is filling their stomach with their meagre income. Wretched clothes, illiteracy, congested living, wrath of rangdars could be seen in almost all parts of the cities of Munger and Bhagalpur.

Provision of Recreation

In the cities of Munger and Bhagalpur cinema houses, Ramlila party, programme of dance, music, theatre and cultural show in terms of exhibitions are common practices which need to be redressed and rearranged for better performance of entertainment. These days the cinema on television has sufficiently reduced the cinegoers in the cinema halls.

Standard of Shopping Centres

The shopping units numbering about 3500 and 4500 respectively in the cities of Munger and Bhagalpur are of very high to medium and poor standard. This happens due to paucity of fund to the business. Although shopkeepers try themselves to arrange the things in a better way but every thing have been done under strain. According to the government record all shops will open at 9 a.m. in the morning and shutters down at about 9 p.m. in the evening. All shopkeepers have to pay tax to the labour office for running a business in the city. On almost all shops huge rush of consumers could be seen from 10 a.m. in the morning up to 7 p.m. in the evening.

Administrative Peace

It has been considered essential for running a business otherwise the fear of rangdars, thieves, dacoits and politicians are always there who like to grab money by force. Without peace no business could prosper. It is essential either by police force or by keeping private guard for the purpose. Especially Nepalese are kept as night guard in the cities of Munger and Bhagalpur.

Conclusion

It may be concluded that there is an integrated impact of several factors on the quality of urban life of people in Munger and Bhagalpur. Some important variables may include terrain conditions, atmospheric elements, types of forest cover, types of land utilization, patterns of crop production, industrial preferment, transport linkages, origin and destination point of buses and concentration of people of different caste, religion, marital status and sex ratio. Here the urban life is very close to the lifestyle of any urban centre especially in Anga plain. Among all the factors the importance of transportation linkage and network is most powerful in attracting people towards these urban centres from the surrounding zone of influence.

REFERENCES

Andrew F.M. and Withey, S.B., (1974), "Developing Measures of Perceived Life Quality: Results from Several National Surveys" in *Journal of Social Indicators Research* Vol. 1, pp. 1-26.

Bauer, R.A. (ed.) (1996), *Social Indicators* (Cambridge).

Dalkey, N.C.; Rourke, D.L.; Lewis, R. and Synder D. (1972), *Studies in the Quality of Life*, (Massachusetts).

Fakhruddin (1991), *Quality of Urban Life*, (Jaipur, Rawat Publications), p. 96.

Jones, D.M. and Flax, M.J. (1970), *The Quality of Life in Metropolitan Washington*, Some Statistical Benchmarks, Washington (1970).

Khola, A. (1974), *Population and Environment* in Bose A., Desai, P.B., Mitra, A. and Sharma J.N. (eds) *Population in India's Development*, (Delhi), pp. 46-47.

Niewiaroski, D.H. (1965), "The level of living of Nations: Meaning and Measurement" in Estadistica: *Journal of the Inter American Statistical Institute*, pp. 3-31.

Northan, R.M. (1979), *Urban Geography* 2nd edition, (New York), p. 93.

Ibid, p.94.

Wilson, J.O. (1969), *Quality of Life in the United States: An Excursion into the new Frontier of Socio-economic Indicators*, (Kansas city).

4 THEORETICAL MODELS OF PSYCHO-SOCIAL CONNOTATIONS OF ECOLOGY AND QUALITY OF LIFE

The world's population is expected to be around 10.5 billion in the year 2110. India's population is estimated to touch the one billion mark by the turn of the century. This would inevitably stretch all facilities and services. Water, food, shelter, health care, education and transport would specially come under a lot of pressure. Along with this would occur the inevitable degradation of the environment. It would also undermine all efforts to improve the quality of life for all human beings. It is being increasingly believed that poverty, crime, depressionalization, international tensions, diseases, injury, destruction and other forms of social pathology, can all be directly linked to population pressure.

Crowding deals with a subjective psychological state when there are too many people in too little a space. The feeling of crowding is negative and has elements of stress. Typically one or many of the following characteristics are associated with crowding. Feeling of discomfort, loss of control over one's environment, lack of privacy, lack of initiative in social interaction, fatigue, boredom etc. Crowding, therefore, has perceptual affective and behavioural consequences. The outcome of such a psychological state is use of strategies that can reduce the feeling of crowding.

Crowding has two aspects to it :

1. *Social Density* : This refers to the number of people in a given space.
2. *Spatial Density* : This refers to the amount of space available for a given number of people.

High level of both these densities are negative and have significant behavioural consequences.

Effects of Overcrowding on Animals

Some recent studies of animal populations in which overcrowding is related to various behavioural pathologies are most suggestive of the stress produced by population density. Calhoun was one of the first to note that disturbances in the territorial and ecological distribution of animals may result in behaviour pathology and physiological malfunctioning. In mice, overcrowding in laboratory cages leads to abnormal sexual behaviour, decreased reproductive and nursing capacities, aborted pregnancies, deficient maternal care for the young and disrupted nest building. Calhoun reared a colony of Norway rats in four different pens, the rats tended to live together in one very-crowded pen. Calhoun coined the pharase "pathological togetherness" to describe this behaviour which lowered the rats' fertility and shortened their lives. Other biologists have observed that mice crowded together in cages display a marked enlargement of the adrenals, a sign of stress; and there have been reports of a high incidence of cannibalism and male importance in crowded mice colonies, adjustive mechanisms which function to keep down population numbers when they rise above a critical point.

It is not possible to dismiss these pathological reactions as unusual phenomena associated with artificial environmental conditions set up in a laboratory, for such behaviour occurs also in natural environments. Deevey has reported on the behaviour of lemmings, rat-like animals found in great abundance in Norway. Approximately every years, when the population becomes excessive for the available territory, there is a mass migration in which huge numbers race blindly to the sea and drown. Such panic lice reactions to overcrowding in laboratory and natural environments are evidence of regulatory mechanisms that enable population control and thereby, survival of the species. Whether extreme overcrowding in human populations produces analogous reactions of stress and social pathology is a moot-point.

Several models of crowding and its consequences on human behaviour have been proposed and/or studied.

Stimulus Overload Model

According to this model, high population density is a stressor as it stimulates the individual, excessively. Too many people in too little space not only crowd the environment about engage in more activities creating more noise, more pollution, more distraction etc. all of which overloads the system. This results in the inability to handle all the incoming information. A consequence of this condition is an aversive feeling. To reduce the overload of stimulation caused by crowding, individuals engage in behaviours that reduce the unavoidable interference from others. At the physical level, the overload leads to fatigue and this is reduced behaviourably by withdrawing. At the cognitive level, since many cognitive stimuli, have to be handled, it results in confusion. Some investigators also regard excessively stimulating environments as causing stress by reducing the attention span, resulting in impaired cognitive functioning. Less friendly and less helpful behaviour seen among city dwellers is an example of such strategy used for coping with stimulus overload. In homes there is greater dissatisfaction among members and desire to spend time outside is more.

Behavioural Constraints Model

High density conditions create stress by imposing restrictions on behavioural freedom. The limitation can produce a psychological reaction whereby the individual is motivated to remove the restriction by either withdrawing or by compensating for the density by engaging in behaviours that help gain control over the environment. For example in a crowded home or hostel people delineate area or seats for themselves (my chair, my corner, my window etc.) as a means of gaining some control over one's crowded environment.

Ecological Model

High density conditions leads to disruptions in accurately understanding the functions of objects in terms of their affordance. All objects in the environment, convey affordances about their functions. For example, a fruit says eat me; a ball says kick me; a baby says protect me etc. These affordances act as cues for adapting to the environments block these affordances resulting in the misreading of the cues regarding their functions. For example, a family which should be perceived as supportive and emotionally positive, due to population density is seen more as a nuisance, rather than a source of joy or support. In such a perceived situation the absence of close-warm feelings among members and the desire to form smaller cliques etc. are easily understandable. Many extended families are not breaking up into separate entities or becoming fully nuclear one of the reasons for this being crowding.

The situation is further compounded by the scarcity of social roles and physical resources. For example, the grandfather plays the senior role member, even through the adult sons have taken over the functions of providers for the family.

The thwarting of such roles and privileges can lead to a feeling of lack of control over one's environment. Behavioural consequences of would be to opt for situations where control over ones environments possible, failing which, the stress is experienced without relief. This can give rise to negative feelings about the family.

Attribution Model

In this model individuals who experience lack of personal space due to crowding and therefore feel the negative attributes the stress to space encroachments. For example, when too many guests arrive and space is short, there is sense of relief when the people leave. However, there are certain situations when high density is not very negatively perceived for example, an enjoyable and voluntary party. So the critical element in response to limitations of space lies in attribution absent; then the sense of crowding is not experienced, so negatively, even though the environment is a high density one.

Stress and Arousal Model

How do high density conditions produce stress? Any physical, social or emotional stimuli that are unsettling can be described as stressful. Stressful conditions are characterized by ·

(a) Stimuli that are very intense.
(b) Beyond the limits of one's control.
(c) Threatening, due to one's inability to cope with it.

High density environments span across these three factors making a stressful situation.

Sources of stress have also been identified :

1. *Physical* : Any intense stimulus arouses stressful psycho-physiological responses. Extreme noises, temperative pain etc. are conditions that cause stress.
2. *Psychological* : Deficiencies in personality make up stress the individuality impeding the progress towards the goal. For example, Inadequate skills, attitudes, poor leadership qualities, having an avoidant personality etc.
3. *Social : Environmental* : Social factors like collective norms traditions etc. can stress the individual by acting a barriers to goal attainment. Environmental factors that stress the individual include, noise, pollution, poor services, over-crowding etc. Stress involves a situation where the individual experiences threat to his important goal and also feels that he is unable to cope with the threat. There is also an impending sense of going to be overwhelmed.

Stresses can arise from major traumatic life events like death of spouse, parent, personal injury, retirement, pregnancy etc., or from the frequent minor hassles of everyday living. Fortunately, traumatic events though extremely stressful, are rare. The minor daily stresses make up for their low intensity be their nagging frequency.

Effects of Stress on Health

Stress affects the physical and psychological health of the individual. It has implications for performance in tasks as well as on social behaviour. The effects of stress on physical health has been well researched. Stress is thought to be silent killer. Medical reports suggest that stress affects health to the tune of 50 to 70 per cent. Stress has been implicated in the occurrence of diseases like heart attacks, hypertension, hardening of the arteries, ulcers and even diabetes. This is because stress renders the immunoligical system inefficient. The more prolonged the stress is, the greater is the threat to the immune system of the body. Studies done on individuals who are in mourning or about to take an important examination have been found to show disruptions in their immune system. However, what is encouraging is, that once these high stress levels are lessened, the restoration of the immune system, is rapid. Stress inevitable arouses the organism.

This us a survival oriented reaction of the organism to meet the emergency situation induced by the stress. The body's resources are then mobilized to meet the threat. This is a demanding and exhausting process. Therefore, if stress is constant or/frequent it takes a toll on the physical health and psychological well-being of the individual. Crowding qualifies as a constant stressor. In order to escape the harmful effects, the individual engages in behaviours that seek to lessen the density and thereby the experience of crowding. Typically, this manifests in the form of less helpful and less friendly behaviours. This can also explain the urban/rural divide in terms of friendliness and feelings for others.

The long-term effects if crowding have shown higher arousal of the system. Arousal is a form of energization of the system. The greater the stress, the greater the arousal. However, adaptation to the stress also occur. But the adaptation generally involves raising the base line. This means that the threshold for stress tolerance becomes lower. Subsequently, in real terms it means that events produce less stress are also, now capable of effecting the organism.

Effects of Crowding on Social Behaviour

Since the effects of high population density are generally negative, it has consequences for social behaviour.

In a study, people who were already in a crowded room were informed that more people are going to come in. The anticipation of more crowding led to feelings of discomfort. It showed up in reduced liking of even fellows waiting alongside. This is seen in a train compartment. Even as the train enters a station the possibility of more people entering produce stress. This leads to overall reduction in friendliness. Significant reduction in helpful behaviour like making room for luggage or staying clear of the passage etc. can be explained in terms of the effects of the crowding.

Individuals who are required to be in environments that are both confining and at the same time be constantly exposed to other individuals as in prisons and other settings like remand homes, free hostels etc. showed greater irritability and reduced satisfaction and harmony in social relationships.

In the community settlement the "Kiffutz" in Israel, where children are raised in community with multiple mothering lacked privacy. This absence of privacy and constant exposure to others resulted in feelings of tension. Anxiety and aggression were some of the other characteristics that were observed.

Students living in three and four seater rooms expressed greater dissatisfaction with their roommates as compared to those living in two seater rooms. The latter also felt less control over their interactions. Some studies have shown that the grades obtained by the students in the more crowded conditions were lower that those from the more comfortable settings. These differences can be attributed to social density. Behaviours that follow, typically involve attempts to reduce the stress and unpleasantness brought about by crowding. Withdrawing and /or less friendly/helpful orientations are the most common forms of response.

Table 4.1 shows the satisfactions derived from roommates in two conditions.

Table 4.1 : Satisfaction with Roommates Under Crowded and Uncrowded Conditions

	Uncrowded	*Crowded*
Satisfaction with roommate	4.9*	3.7
Perceived cooperativeness of roommate	4.7*	3.9

* Higher number indicate mere positive responses (Based on data from Baron *et al.*, 1976).

The lowered frequency of interaction in high density places can be seen as the affects of less attraction for neighbours. This can then be attributed to crowding whereby lessening of contacts is a way of ensuring reducing the unpleasantness of crowding.

Although it appears that high density leads to lower attraction, there is evidence that under conditions of high spatial density, this response is more characteristic of male and females. In an experiment male and female subjects participated in same—sex groups of six. Consistent findings on a variety of measures indicated that while males responded more negatively to group members in high than in low spatial density conditions, females, liked group members more under high density conditions.

They state that while both males and females experience arousal from high density, social norms permit females to share their distress with others in their group, which leads to liking distress with others in their group, which leads to liking and cohesion. The same norms prohibit males from sharing stress, which causes a more negative response. In a follow-up experimental, 1976, it was found that when females were not permitted to interact with each other, their positive reactions to high density were limited.

Pro-social Behaviour : If high density leads to lower attraction and to withdrawal responses, how might it affect helping? For examples, suppose you lost a contact lens or something else of value.

Where would you be most confident of finding someone who would help you look for it; in a high-rise or a low-rise building? In a large city or in a small city? Interestingly, most research on how density affects pro-social behaviour has been done in field setting like these. In fact, one set up studies has compared helping in building characterized by high and low density, and a second has compared pro-social acts in large cities and small cities.

In studies that explored helping as a function of building density, it was found consistently that greater density leads to less helping.

Studies compared pro-social acts in high, medium, and low-density dormitories. Envelopes, which were stamped and address, were dropped in the dormitories, and helpfulness was measured by the number that were picked up and placed in the mail. The results showed that 58 per cent were mailed in the high density condition, 79 per cent in the medium density condition, and 88 per cent in the low density condition. In an interesting corroborative study, the effect of social density on compliance with a prosocial request (printed on signs) for cafeteria users to return their trays to designated areas. It was found that fewer users complied during high density periods (Table 4.2).

Table 4.2 : Mean Scores on the Feeling of Crowding and Social Behaviour for Outside-Inside Density Groups

Groups		*Mean*	*df*	*t*
Outside	High density	61.00	98	49
	Low density	60.00		
Inside	High density	89.00	48	7.49*
	Low density	46.70		

* $p<.01$

The second line of research, which compared urban and rural helping, provides more equivocal evidence concerning a density—pro-social behaviour relationship. In one group of studies it was found that city dwellers were less helpful and less informative to strangers than rural dwellers. Urbanities were less likely to admit a stranger who needed to use a telephone, less likely to assist a caller who mistakenly called a wrong number, less who had mistakenly called a wrong number, less likely to correct over payments in making change, and less likely to report theft than rural dwellers.

A num'ber of interesting field studies have shown that resident of low-rise buildings are more willing to help other than residents of high-rise buildings.

Withdrawal : Withdrawal may be associated with high levels of social contact. Studies have found that withdrawal may function as an anticipatory response to high density, as a means of coping the ongoing high density, and as an after effect. For example, the mere expectation of high social density elicits withdrawal responses, including lower levels of eye contact, head movements away from others and maintenance of greater interpersonal distances. Withdrawal also occurs during ongoing high density interactions : Subjects are more willing to discuss intimate topics under low density conditions, and both children and psychiatric patients interact less frequently as room density increase. Finally, it appears that withdrawal can constitute an after effect of exposure to density. Males were less likely to volunteer for another experimental session after high social density and groups of males preferred larger personal space and recalled fewer names after exposure to high density.

Aggression : If density can make people less helpful or want to withdraw; then it is possible that density can also lead to hurting behaviours.

Many studies have also established greater aggression and hostility from high population areas. Apart from crowding the high density areas like the slums, require that people have to complete for scarce resources also e.g. Space, water etc. Hostilities can break out frequently in these conditions because they have conditions which are highly tension producing.

Competition is a major possible source of interpersonal conflict. This conflict can easily become inter-group conflict under conditions that threaten limited vital resource. These would be heightened by feelings of insecurity due to dissatisfaction of needs, resulting from population pressures.

One study is tallisled that moderately high-density conditions led to increased aggression in males, while very low and very high-density conditions led to decreased aggressiveness. In another conditions led to decreased aggressiveness. In another study, aggression was found to increase in boys under conditions of high density. These findings can be explained in terms of competition for limited resources which males, more aggressive as a group. Sex differences have been observed with respect to aggression. Same sex groups of eight members were placed in a room that was either large or small. Males rated themselves as more aggressive in the small rooms as compared to females.

Studies of boys and girls in the classroom as well as in anticipation of more cordoned, produced more aggression among males. Spatial density, rather than social density seems to have aggressive outcomes from males.

Inside and outside conditions of population density and its effects on social behaviour were studied. It was found that density is a necessary but not a sufficient condition for producing feeling of crowding.

But high density within the house had significant effect on the feeling of crowding. Table 4.3 gives a comparison of the behaviour feelings of individual living in high low-density conditions.

Table 4.3 : Social Behaviours and the Feelings of Crowding Experienced by the Residents of High and Low Inside Density Conditions

Behaviour Feeling	*Density*	*Mean*	*t(48)*
Crowding	High	3.55	3.33*
	Low	1.82	
Privacy	High	3.07	
	Low	1.38	3.07*
Physical condition	High	3.22	
	Low	1.44	4.45*
Interaction	High	3.24	
	Low	1.38	3.20*
Neighbours	High	2.65	
	Low	1.69	3.92*
Insecurity	High	2.67	
Illness	High	3.44	
	Low	1.71	3.39*
Withdrawal	High	3.88	
	Low	2.46	2.43*

* $p<.01$

Further, crowding affected health, feelings of security, privacy and generally produced the desire to leave. Negative moods and dislike for affiliation were also related to crowding inside the house.

The feelings of crowding in high and low socio-economic studies groups have been compared, and are given in Table 4.4.

Table 4.4 : The Feeling of Crowding in High and Low Economic Status Groups

Dimensions of the Feelings of Crowding	*Economic Status*	*Mean*	*t (48)*
Comfortable-	High	1.97	
Uncomfortable	Low	2.34	2.64
Good-bad	High	1.98	
	Low	2.48	3.57*
High congestion	High	2.02	
Low congestion	Low	2.14	0.32
Happy-sad	High	2.08	
	Low	2.48	2.85*
Pleasant-unpleasant	High	1.86	
	Low	2.40	4.00*
Positive-negative	High	1.86	
	Low	2.36	3.57*

* $p<.05$

Table 4.5 shows the feeling of crowding under high and low density conditions in terms several dimensions.

Table 4.5 : The Feeling of Crowding in High and Low Economic Status Groups

Dimensions of the Feelings of Crowding	*Economic Status*	*Mean*	*t (48)*
Comfortable-	High	2.32	
Uncomfortable	Low	2.00	2.57
Good-bad	High	2.40	
	Low	2.04	2.57*
High congestion- Low congestion	High	2.00	
	Low	2.14	0.81
Happy-sad	High	2.38	
	Low	2.18	1.42*
Pleasant-unpleasant	High	1.86	
	Law	1.98	2.14*
Positive-negative	High	2.25	
	Low	2.10	1.07*

* $p<.05$

The Jain finding show that high density in itself does not lead to low degree of attraction towards neighbours; but density conditions can aggravate aversive feelings if space and resources are extremely limited and have to be shared. This finding has implications for architectural and colony features that have to be kept in mind while designing high density housing localities.

In the Indian societal conditions where emotional bonds between relatives, neighbours and community have been traditionally emphasized; the western models which predict low interpersonal attraction in high density areas, cannot be fully observed. In fact in highdensity areas, cannot be fully observed. In fact it is, the high socio-economic class who are also highly competitive and show less interpersonal attraction for neighbours and others, as compared to the lower socio-economic group. The typical helping out relatives, neighbours etc in times of funerals, weddings etc. is more characteristics of highly populated, lower economic group. The results thus show that economic factors interact with high density and societal values of moderate the effects of high density living conditions on social behaviours.

Effects of High Density on Task Performance

One of the most critical questions that can be asked about high density is whether it affects task performance. The answer has important implications for the design of all types of living and working spaces (e.g., schools, factories). Most early studies used simple tasks and were consistent in finding no decrements under high social to spatial density. As seen in the table below both high social and high spatial density, led to decrements in complex maze task performance, but these decrements were more pronounced under conditions of high social density. In a field setting, also decrements in complex task performance, but these decrements were more pronounced under conditions of high social density. In a feld setting, also decrements in complex task performance over time in overcrowded dormitory rooms (three persons in a room built for two) were observed (Table 4.6).

Table 4.6 : Errors in Maze Performance as a Function of Spatial Density and Social Density

Low spatial density	34.20
High spatial density	37.44
Low social density	32.13
High social density	39.50

In another study poorer complex task performance under crowded conditions was noticed, but there was no impairment in simple task performance. Even anticipation of crowding led to poorer complex task performance.

The differential effects of high-density conditions on single and complex tasks can be explained using the concept of arousal. Arousal when moderate has the properties of being a motivator. But when the organism in over aroused as in the case of overcrowding, the anxiety is experienced. Anxiety is detrimental to learning and performance. Complex tasks which need greater attention and problem-solving capabilities is more adversely affected than simple tasks. So high density is more adverse for complex task performance than simple tasks.

When high density conditions prevail and the expectations of task performance are also low; it yields significantly poorer functioning.

In another study interaction among members was found to be an important factor that produces lowering of tasks performance in a high density condition.

Table 4.6 shows the effect of interaction and density related task performance.

Interaction is necessary for density-related task performance deficits to occur (Adapted from Heller, Groff, and Soloman, 1977).

A final and very important question is whether high density can cause aftereffects, as well as immediate effects, on performance. As you will recall, noise is a stressor that has been linked to consequences occurring after exposure, and some studies suggest that crowding has lingering effects as well. For example, it was found that subjects exposed to high density later showed less persistence at working on unsolvable puzzles than subjects exposed to low density. In as attempt to determine whether perceived control would lessen after effects, some subjects had the option of leaving a crowded room to complete the study in a spacious setting (i.e., perceived control). Although no one took advantage of the option, this group showed fewer aftereffects than the group that wasn't offered an opportunity to leave. The similarity of these findings to those with noise effects further suggests that noise and high density may affect people in similar ways.

Performance suffering under high density, can also be explained as stress induced. Stress has been found to systematically lower performance primarily because it distracts the person from concentrating on the task on hand. Lack of the concentration in turn is because of the unpleasantness of the experience. This shift in focus from task to the negative emotions reduces efficiency. Complex tasks

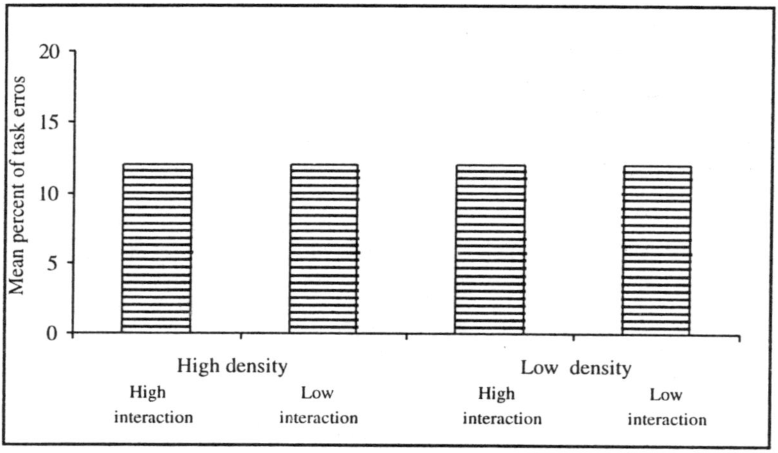

Fig. 4.1 : Interaction and Density Relates Task Performance

stand to be more readily disrupted by stress as these require greater concentration and therefore stiffer larger deficits.

Decision-making under conditions of stress have been described as resulting in bad choices. The strategies utilized in problem-solving under stress conditions have been found to be poor. Many premature decisions are also associated with choices made under stress. Scanning of the possible alternatives for making decisions has been found to be disorganized under conditions of stress. A tendency to close the issue on hand as quickly as possible is linked to the presence of stress. Here the individual is motivated to overcome the aversiveness of the stress and therefore quickly engages in action to reduce it. Premature closure without considering all aspects of a given situation results, owing to the stress effects.

Crowding not only induces stress and thereby lowers performance but can also be implicated in poorer decisions and premature closures. Crowding also introduces the stimulus overload condition. To reduce the overload, individuals enagage in hasty and ill-conceived decisions.

Moderate levels of stress which have motivational properties of energizing the organism, has significant positive features, in terms of performances. Medium amounts of stress are considered as arousing the organism to better performance through increased mobilization of energy and better intentional focus.

However, when they cross the optimal conditions, then the effects are negative and adversely affect performance. Crowding, due to its excessive stimulating features, qualifies more as a stressor and thereby has deleterious consequences on performance.

The only kind of skills that are not very adversely affected are the well established ones like drinking, swimming, playing an instrument or speaking a language.

Crowding as a stressor has significant effects on the health of the individual. This in turn has negative consequences for learning and performance.

Since the effects of crowding on health is also infavourable, performance can also suffer on account of reduced health in an indirect manner.

The effect of stress on learning is even more disruptive. Learning involves the acquisition of a new set of responses. This implies that the correct response exists at the 0 per cent level of probability of occurring. This low probability response is at the bottom of the hierarchy. Learning means pushing this 0 per cent probability response to one of 100 per cent probability. Such an endeavour requires high degrees of attention and cognitive inputs. Stress induced by crowding, arouses the organism and such an arousal state is energizing. When learning is engaged in this energized condition, the first natural response to occur is a previously learnt 100 per cent probability one. The new response (to be acquired) has to now compete with the well established earlier response. By the very nature of the process, the newer response has disadvantage and would therefore surer, seriously.

Research evidence shows that even the mere presence of others is deleterious to learning.

Crowding (which is the presence of many people) would lower learning not only because of the presence of others, but so because of too many people. Thus, stress induced by crowding would hampar learning in an even more pronounced manner. The new responses to be learnt would in the competition with the older established ones, get depressed easily. So greater effort and attention would be required to offset this condition. Stress in such a context is clearly debilitating.

Education imparte in high density classrooms is found to be ineffective. Further, children who study in classes with large numbers, are also more likely to come from homes that are crowded, than otherwise. This would suggest that both the conditions are unfavourable for promoting learning to that extra would have to be made for reasonable levels of learning to occur. In such strained conditions, students would also not readily have role models of sustained learners. To compound it, other stressors would be in operation in such disadvantaged environments. All these together pose a set of factors that are not conducive to serious learning activities. This could well be the explanation for the absence of children from the slum sections benefiting from long-term education.

Effects of Crowding on Motivation

Crowding inevitably leads to greater competition for both space as well as resources. If competition is continuous, it can produce increased tolerance for competition according to Uday Jain, who has done pioneering work on crowding in India.

Scarcity of resources typically manifests in struggle for power with a view to cornering the scant resources.

In India, the immense desire for power is not so much for power itself but because power symbolizes to access to resources. Obtaining railway tickets, getting admissions in educational institutions, jobs, telephone connections, licenses for business and industry, etc., are all related to power as a means of need gratification.

In Jain's study it was clearly demonstrated that high density situation lead to greater competitiveness as a way to obtaining the available resources. Urban people form high density areas showed more competition tolerance than the low density areas. Similarly, the high-density urban individuals competed more than the density rural individuals. High and low density areas in the rural setting also yielded similar results.

In this situation of competing for scarce resources, people hardly find time to think or be mindful of others' needs. This can account for the apparent indifference of the present day city dweller. Given that one has limited time/energy, etc. for obtaining some benefits for oneself, expecting one to be very caring considerate to others seems to be a very unreasonable one. The blanket statement made about the younger generation perhaps needs to be reinterpreted using the concepts of high levels of competition generated by high levels of population. It is a clear that the earlier generation competed less for the resources, as there was a large amount that could be shared.

If competition becomes fierce as the population increases, it is possibly that the individual's interpersonal relationships would be markedly affected. The biggest causality of such a condition would be consideration for others.

Studies show that there are urban/rural differences in the extent to which they tolerate competition. Greater tolerate for competition has also been associated with the need patterns of the high and the low competitive individuals. Low competitiveness is associated with helpful and considerate behaviours while high competitiveness is related to order, neatness, organization, etc. the laters needs are likely to be more readily disrupted in a crowded environment. Hence, the reduced consideration and helping behaviour found among the high competitive individuals can be easily attributed to their negative perceptions of others who are viewed as rivals. This is due to the fact that too many persons would not only increase the competition but also intrude into their neat and orderly styles of functioning. Such a situation would naturally yield less consideration and helpful behaviour.

High density dwellers have to encounter vast numbers in their daily activities. They try to conserve their psychic energy by keeping interaction to the barest possible number of people. In such a context, friendly, helpful and considerate social interactions are highly unlikely. This is more clear among the more educated who are more competitive and thus uninterested in nurturing supportive and thus uninterested in nurturing supportive behaviours with others with any degree of spontaneity.

So, the explorations of several density behaviour relationships shows that high density has various kinds of negative effects.

High density is like any other potential stress and it has

1. Immediate effects, such as physiological arousal and negative states.
2. Coping responses like withdrawal, aggression etc.
3. After-effects and cumulative effects like health and performance.
4. Motivational consequences (increased tolerance for competition).

All these models are overlapping and are supplementary in terms of explaining the stress experienced crowding and the behavioural consequences that follow, being stress-alleviating in nature.

Table 4.7 : Summary of Theoretical Perspective on Crowding

Conceptual Approach	*Critical Cause(s) of Crowding*	*Primary Coping Mechanisms*
Social Overload Social stimulation	Excessive social contact too much	Escape stimulation; prioritize input and disregard low priorities withdrawal
Behaviour constraint	Reduced behavioural freedom	Aggressive behaviour leave situation coordinate actions with other
Unwanted interaction	Excessive unarguable or unwanted contact with others	Withdrawal; organization of small primary groups
Interference	Disruption or blocking of goal-directed behaviour	Create structure aggression; escape
Ecological resources	Scarcity of boundaries	Defence of group exclusion of outsiders

Recent conceptualizations on the effect of high density revolve around two concepts control and privacy.

Perceived control is regarded as potent mediator of stress.

When we believe that we can control a stressor or other aspects of a situation, the aversiveness of stress appears to be reduced. It follows that even if no other problems are apparent, losing or not having control can also be stressful. Several researchers have proposed that high density can cause a loss of control (or prevent some one from ever having control) and that this loss of control is the primary mechanism by which density causes stress.

Can we really explain the negative effects of high density as a loss of control? The answer is "Yes", even though at times the explanation seems a little strained. Some explanations fit well the notion of unwanted interaction is a control-based perspective. Negative effects are the result of contact that is too frequent which makes control over when, where and with whom people interact difficult to maintain. As a result, interactions become unpredictable and frequently unwanted. The behaviour constraint notion is also control-based, describing high density as eliminating behavioural options and reducing freedom to behave as one might like. For example, having inadequate space can constrain out behaviour by making it impossible to control the nature the degree of intimacy in one-on-one interactions by adjusting the distance we stand from people but in a very crowded room we may find ourselves with no choice—we must stand close to people whether we know them well or not. In this manner, we can lose control over intimacy regulation.

Interference can also be viewed as a threat to control as our attempts to achieve one or another goal are repeatedly blocked or disrupted. And resource problems the focus of ecological models, can limit our choices and restrict our ability to exercise control. To some extent, all of these consequences of high density that have been related to negative effects do cause a reduction in control. But, is there any direct research evidence for the relation between density and control?

Research examination the links between high density and loss of control has taken two different tracks. The first has been to manipulate personal control (provide some subjects and not others with perceived control) and see if it has any effect on experience in high density settings. Example subjects response to riding in an elevator crowded with confederate of the experimenter. They observed a tendency for people to gravitate toward the elevator floor selection panel (a control panel, if you will), so they manipulated whether subjects were able to stand near to (high control condition) or not (low control condition). The results indicated that subjects standing near the panel felt better than those in a different corner. They also thought that the elevator was larger than subjects not near the panel.

A somewhat different approach found that noise was associated with negative after effects, which was reduced when subjects had some degree of control over the noise. A similar, study with density instead of noise was carried out. Once again, negative after effects were associated with stress when control was not available. Subjects who had more perceived control, on the other hand, did not exhibit negative after effects were associated with stress when control was not available. Subjects who had more perceived control, on the other hand, did not exhibit negative after effects following exposure to high density.

In a high density condition in the laboratory, subjects had varying degrees of control over the setting. Those with control felt better than those without. These studies demonstrate that control can reduce the effects of high density relative to no-control, high-density experiences. They do not, however, demonstrate that high density itself has consequences similar to those associated with loss or lack of control.

However, studies conducted in field settings found that chronically high residential density was associated with helplessness like behaviour. Learned helplessness is a syndrome in which people who are exposed to uncontrollable setting learn that they cannot control the setting, and hence stop trying to do so. This manifests itself in reduced motivation and cognitive activity. Subjects, who were children and adolescents showed symptoms of helplessness that were associated with density in their homes.

Symptoms of helplessness were also found among people exposed to high density in their residential environment over prolonged periods. More recently this has been directly linked to perceptions of control in residential settings, their behaviour become increasingly like that associated with helplessness.

All of these studies taken together suggest that control is involved in negative high density effects. When control is available, high density has less impact on people than when it is not available. Further chronic exposure to high density appears to be associated with learned helplessness.

Crowding in the Home and in the Schools

Imagine yourself growing up in a small apartment with five other people who are continuously interacting with each other and with you. With so many people in so little space, you may grow up to feel the world is a complex place in which you have little power to influence events (What consequences does this have? When we come to believed we cannot control our outcomes by responding appropriately (as may result from living in high density conditions), we no longer perform effectively in a number of situations. This syndrome is called "learned helplessness".

Two interesting and provocative studies demonstrated the relationship between residential density and susceptibility to "learned helplessness". In one experiment it was found that children who lived in high density conditions were less likely than those in low density to try to control the administration of rewards they were to receive. In a second experiment subjects from both groups to an initial frustration task on which responses and outcomes were non-contingent children from high density homes did significantly worse on a subsequent task for which outcomes were contingent. Thus it appears that home density is an important determinant of both the use of control and performance after frustrating non-contingent reward situations.

Besides the home environment what other settings may be source of 'learned helplessness'? One important culprit may be the schools. As classroom size increases, learned helplessness training begins to occur. The argue that larger classroom sizes lead to lower student expectations for control of reinforcement, because teacher feedback concerning student work becomes less discriminative. For example, as class size goes up, individualized student-teacher interactions decrease, and generalized (rather than individualized) praise and criticism increase. Clearly such conditions could lead to a state of learned helplessness with its negative consequences for performance. This could have profound consequences for learning.

An alternative to the density-intensity model has been proposed by Freedman. He agrues that density only intensifies reactions that would occur in any case in a particular situation. High density according to him, heightens the importance of other people and magnifies out reactions to them. Thus high density would intensify the aversiveness of an unpleasant situation and intensify the pleasantness of positive situations. From this point of view, a number of factors can lead to a negative reaction in a high-density situation.

One of the benefits of such a model, which utilizes the notion of intensification; is the link between crowding and contagion. Contagion is the rapid spread of behaviours or emotions from one person to the group. For example, people coming back after viewing a game. The negative effect (if the home team loses) would be quickly passed on among all those returning.

This model provides a framework that specifies three factors as important in determining the experience of crowding. They are :

1. Individual difference.
2. Situational conditions.
3. Social conditions.

Identifying individual difference variables can help determine who among the selected persons will be more sensitive to the constraint of space. Studies have already established gender differences in the aversire feelings, due to crowding.

Some persons prefer to sit for away from others while others prefer to sit closer. This can also affect the degree to which crowding is experienced.

Personality characteristics also moderate our reactions to high density. It has been found that internals (who feel they control their fate) display a higher threshold of crowding than externals (who feel events are controlled by outside forces). The primary problems encountered in high individual differences are important. People who screen themselves from interaction and organize their surroundings were better able to cope with social density than were people who did not screen themselves. One would expect that this variable would be less important when spatial problem were paramount.

A final individual difference variable that has been linked to reactions to high density is one's adaptation level (from past experience under high density conditions). A number of investigators have hypothesized that people with history of high density living are less likely to experience crowding in a novel situation than are people with a history of isolation. For example, it has been found that the Japanese, residents of Hong Kong and the Logoli (all of whom live under extremely high density) have developed social mechanisms that may be viewed as adaptive for high density living.

In addition to being moderated by individual difference variables, our reactions to high density are also affected by situational conditions. An important situational condition is the degree of control we have. Complementing those discussed earlier, several additional studies have found that allowing people increased control over a situation leads to less perceived crowding. The applied potential for introducing control in high density conditions, is phenomenal. For example, Individuals living in high density situations, can be given training for enhancing control, i.e. how to share space and ensure privacy. This is bound to help alleviate crowding and it negative effects.

Other situational factors as whether we are in a primary environment (like a home) or a secondary environment (like a restaurant), and the extent to which other stressors, such as noise etc. are involved, also affect crowding. When we are in a primary environment we may be more likely to experience crowding. Finally, in terms of activities there is suggestive evidence that we are more likely to experience crowding when engaged in work, rather than in recreation. Life styles that increase social contacts like picnics, games travel etc. are more likely to generate feelings of crowding in dense environments than life styles that decrease the likelihood of social contacts.

In addition to individual differences and situational conditions, social conditions can be manipulated to affect whether or not we are crowded. These are variables that make up the social "climate" of a high density situation such as the degree of friendship and the level of social interference and interaction. For example, our relationship with the people crowding is experienced with liked rather than disliked others and with acquaintances than with strangers. To the extent that we experience social interference (interruptions) by others or excessive proximity or intimacy (too direct eye contact or body orientation) crowding is more likely. Finally crowding is more often experienced in unstructured task situations than in structured ones.

High density within primary groups (e.g. families) has repeatedly shown fewer effects than it has in other groups when density within apartment units in examined, for example it appears to be negligible as a factor associated with illness or behavioural difficulties. Degree of acquaintance and relative position of an individual in a group's dominance hierarchy also affects crowding. The presence of friends or the possession of high status tends to blunt the aversiveness of large numbers of people or cramped spaces.

Since some of the conditions and factors that mediated the experience of crowding have been delineated; it is worth considering how one can modify existing environments or plan new ones to mitigate the effects of crowding.

Some Architectural Modifications

To begin with, greater ceiling height is associated with a feeling of less crowding. Rectangular rooms seems to elicit lass crowding than square rooms, of the same area. Rooms that have visual escapes such as doors or windows are rated less crowded than rooms that do not have such escapes. The addition of flexible partitions in rooms, lessens feelings of crowding. Increasing the brightness of room by providing suitable wall colours leads to less perceived crowding. The presence of visual distracters, e.g. pictures, some movement etc. also helps reduce crowding. Finally, studies that have evaluated the aversive effects of Social versus Spatial density have established that social density is more negative than spatial density. Architects and designers must address themselves to the fact that too many people produce greater sense of crowding than too little space.

Architectural Design for Crime Prevention

Cries are the hotled of crimes of different kinds owing to a peculiar mix of people, social physical and housing factors. Large scale rural to urban migration; the concentration of the underprivileged in core urban areas, crowding of population into higher and higher densities all significantly affect life styles environmental conditions and crime rates, in the large metropolitan areas.

It is now becoming increasingly clear that the physical and architectural designs of residential environments can elicit attitudes and behaviour from residents, which contribute in a major way towards insuring their security. Residential environments with certain physical features have crime-inhibiting qualities.

As a starter, 'semi-private' spaces should be 'designed in' to facilitate social interaction between residents and thus encourage the development of social order. Such areas should exist both inside and outside the building and should exist both inside and outside the building and should be planned so as to make pleasant social interactions inevitable. This is especially true of many Asian countries and particularly India, where dependence and interdependence rather than independence is a valued social goal in interpersonal relationships. Many homes have extended families, which involve the living together of many individuals of different generations. So our housing colonies should be totally designed to suit our socio-cultural environmental therefore needs. So houses that alienate cannot be appropriate for India. Yet, colonies that grow up where spaces are 'nobodys' can become dumping ground easy for encroachments or neglect and subtly support crime and randalism.

In order to take care of this situation the design of a 'defensible space' has been proposed. This notion implies that building should be so designed that all the space appears to 'belong' to some individual or group. Such areas can be easily depended and therefore promote surveillance and thus reduce unauthorized activities and crime.

In order to take care of this situation the design of a 'defensible space' has been proposed. This notion implies that building should be so designed that all the space appears to 'belong' to some individual or group. Such areas can be easily depended and therefore promote surveillance and thus reduce unauthorized activities and crime.

In practice this means that areas around buildings e.g. service lanes, parks, playgrounds etc. must belong to the building. Then these

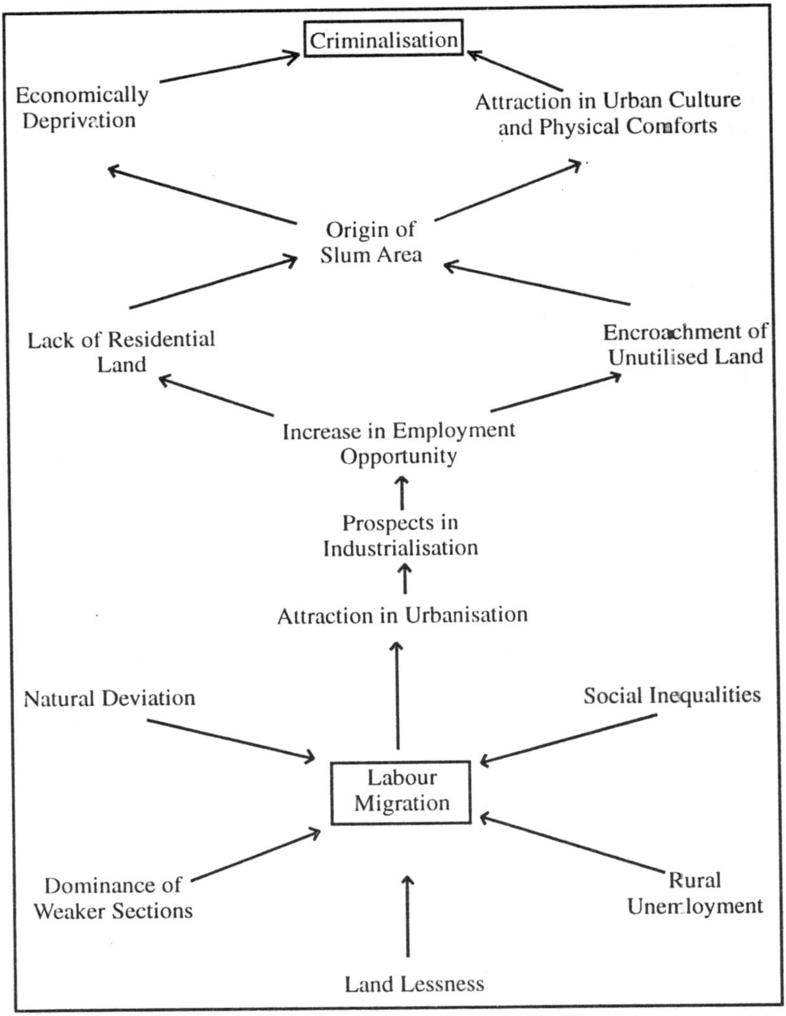

Fig. 4.2 : Crime in Slum Area and Tentative Design for Their Prevention

areas would be perceived by both the residents of the building and outsiders as extensions of the building. The other side of this issue is that public areas such as hallways, corridors, stairways etc., should be eliminated as far as possible. This can be done through horizontal rather than vertical constructions.

Where this is not possible the open 'air spaces' like courtyards combined porches or hallways that are accessible to only a small group of residents should be constructed. These designs would facilitate territorial functioning. If corridors have to be provided; they can be made to run along the window side. This is easy to be monitored.

Designs should also help police surveillance. Often buildings are not open to police viewing or even reaching at times of need. All residential housing units should have a garbage dump, a community centre and a self-monitoring cell. It should be the responsibility of a duly elected group of representatives to keep their environment clean, green and protected.

A Look to the Future

A national and regional regulation regarding acceptable levels of density should be evolved and stringently enforced. To insure lower population density, attitudinal and behavioural change at the individual level should be taken by the government on war footing in a massive scale. Considering the destructive potential of overpopulation, it is time to rethink many of our beliefs concerning proper family size.

REFERENCES

Alexander, F.G. and Selesnick, S.T. (1996), *The History of Psychology*. New York : Harper & Row.

Bandura, A., (1973), *Aggression : A Social Learning Analysis*. Englewood Cliffs, N.J. : Printice-Hall.

Baum, A. (1998), Disasters, Natural and Otherwise, *Psychology Today*, 22, pp. 56-60.

Berkman, L.F., & Syme, S.L. (1979), Social Networks, Host Resistance, and Mortality : A Nine Year Followup Study of Alameda County Residents. *American Journal of Epidemiology*, 109, 186-204.

Cohan, S. (1978), Environmental Load and Allocations of Attentions. In A. Baum. J. E. Singer and S. Valins (Eds.), *Advances in Environmental Psychology* (Vol. I, pp. 1-29), Hillsdale, N.J. : Erlabaum.

Harrel, J.P. (1980), Psychological Factors and Hypertension : A Status Report, *Psychological Bulletin*, 87, 482-501.

Krantz, D.S. *et al.* (1987), Stress and Type a Behaviour : Interactions Between Environmental and Biological Factors. In A.V. Baum & J.E. Singer (Eds) *Hardware of Psychology and Health* (Vol. 5) Hillsdate, N.J. Eribaum.

Peveler, R.C. & Johnston, D.W. (1986), Subjective and Cognitive Effects of Relaxation, *Behaviour Reseach and Therapy*, 24, 413-419.

Prient, R.G. (1998), Benzodiazepines : The Search for Tranquility. In M.J. Chrisbel & P.G. Mellett (Eds.), *The Psychosonation Approach : Centempcrary Practice of Whole-Person Care*, New Yourk : Willey.

Selye, H. (1976), *The Stress of Life* (Revised Edition) New York : Mc Graw-Hill.

Shadiro, J.L., (1987), The Expectant Father, *Psychology Today*, 21. pp. 36-42.

Zimbardo, P.G., (1988), *Psychology and Life* (12th ed.) Glenview, IL: Scott, Foreman.

5 CONCEPTUAL VIEW OF QUALITY OF URBAN LIFE

The concept urban life can be stated as spatial relationship of urban development, environmental relations of different events, size, shape and levels of living standards of urban people. Firstly, the spatial relationship deals with the site and situation of quality of urban life and their variations from place to place due to the variations in facilities available to the residents at a place. In urban area housing unit, an urbanite, an industry, an urban institution, a shopping unit, transport linkages and educational institutions from the duality of urban life. Now-a-days, even play grounds, recreational centres, cinema houses, studio, banking facilities, post office, telephone office, life insurance offices and administrative centres encompasses the spatial location of urban activities.

Secondly, the concept of environmental relations determine why and how at a particular place the retail and wholesale business have flourished. Because only those places are considered fit for at urban activities where at least the optimum threshold of consumers must be available by the urban centres of Munger and Bhagalpur. In place, the business proposition is sure to die out. In case of surplus turn. Over of customers at a particular shop for the purchase of particular type of good, the expansion of such shopping activities would be beneficial. Besides, these capital incentive, facilities of transport, street frontage, administrative peace and business efficiency account for the quality of urban life.

A housing and shopping unit is a product of the cultural advancement of people in the process of economic development of the urban society in order to maintain a happy and prosperous life by purchasing and selling of goods. In this way, the shop is an emblem of urban culture and living normal life. It is an example of getting together geographical, commercial as well as economic aspects of the urban society even if shopping activity is a non-productive function.

Thirdly, the conceptual view of urban life includes the population size of urban place and the functional magnitude of the centre including population served and area served. In such a situation the number of shopping units, congregation of persons at a place, areal expansion of the urban centre and magnitudes of trade area determined with the help of demarcation of the zone of influence of the urban centre may determine the size. This generally includes surrounding area of the urban centre is functional magnitude of the city and the demarcation of hinterland. So far as the periodicity of retail business is concerned the shopping business generally runs under a shade or inside house in front of a road for 24 hours only in case the site is basically defensible from the onslaught of thieves, anti-social elements, hazards of climate and environmental pollution and the availability of labourers and customers as well.

Under the concept of consumer behaviour the trip behaviour of consumers available from the urban and the rural areas for the purchase of consumer goods is considered along with the distance travelled, area served, agricultural and industrial productivity of the region and the demand for particular goods and services, including accessibility of a place.

The quality of urban life has been the product of location, time, space and principles of the function concerned.

In analysing the sample of urban life the study of floor space, turn out of customers, input of capital in a shop, height of the building, workers engaged in service facilities, volume of the sale of goods, slums and squatter settlements, urban misery and rural misery and rural poverty are all meaningful concepts to be considered. This may be regarded as a case study in which a representative item has been chosen far a detailed analysis through the stochastic process. Here, the study of house plans, front space and the function of a shop along with other details are considered.

The concept of urban region and regionalism has been aimed to divide into a number of urban regions and the integrated study is known as regional view in terms of the area confined for the location of medicine shops, grocery shops, cloth shops, tea stalls, hotels, embroidery shops, readymade stores, grain store, book stalls and others. In this way, the integrated study of all these items is known as regional concept. Scenes and sceneries and people behaviour in fringe area of the city and city centre are quite different from one-another and all these come under the purview of regionalism.

Here, the discussion concentrates on theoretical concepts of the growth and developments of the towns of Munger and Bhagalpur in the state of Bihar. This notion is correct as the development of commercial agriculture in a massive way and the majority of workers in such cities are engaged in primary sector and the development of city is against the norms of primary and tertiary sectors as one believes in cultivation of land while the others are shopping and industrial activities.

So far as the site and situation of Munger and Bhagalpur are concerned they are located in extreme agricultural belt, where the majority of population is engaged in non-agricultural operations. Although in recent years the literate persons going away from agriculture work, which is a sad state of affairs as, the white collar job is difficult to get for the entire population.

Conceptual Model of the City

It is an interaction between primary, secondary and tertiary functions. Here, the mobility of workers from primary to secondary may be for the welfare of the society, primary to tertiary for better income and from secondary to tertiary for modernity and enhance the status of the society (Fig. 5.1).

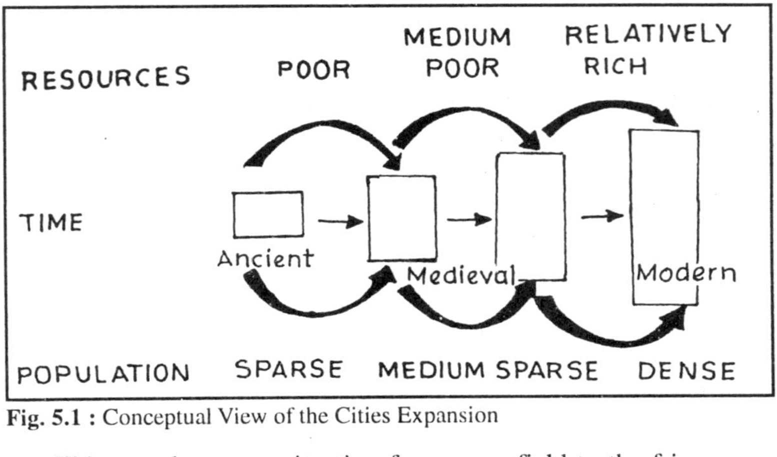

Fig. 5.1 : Conceptual View of the Cities Expansion

This may be a true situation from open field to the fringe area industrial sectors and again from fringe area to the central part of the city. Only old and retired people move from the central market towards the rural settlements located near the fringe of the market.

It has also been observed that the main thorough fare of almost all villages in the hinterland of the cities of Munger and Bhagalpur arranged towards the towns are found in the nearby area. These are some of the conceptual backgrounds, which favour the growth, and development of the cities of Munger and Bhagalpur.

Urbanization is the aggregation of people into large, dense and heterogeneous human settlements. It also serves as the spatial manifestation of the urban process. Actually, town is the visible result of two processes, which combine and interact to form the composite urban process. The first of these processes leads to the evolution of a social and cultural organization, which is initially a sub-system but eventually becomes the dominant system in a given society. This process incorporates a growing proportion of the total population into the urban social structure, while changing lifestyles, which continually modify and transform the urban social structure. This is the process, where by an increasing proportion of the total population is incorporated into urban settlement patterns, giving rise to the town as a basic ecological frame work for social life and production, which in turn leads to its expansion and transformation in geographic space.

The evolutionary patterns of urban growth on the landscape are of fundamental importance in location theory. From the time when Von Thunen and Weber propounded the concepts of agricultural location and industrial location respectively, the investigation into distributional aspects and spatial interrelationships of urban settlements has received increasing attention of the location theorist. In his study of the relations between primary agricultural production and markets, Von Thunen contributed both to the basis for Christaller's central place theory and to the model building methodology. Working on the pattern of farming in North Germany and adjacent regions in the early Nineteenth Century he developed a model of the location of agricultural production based on distance and marginal productivity of land. He was interested in land-use pattern, which would develop under the given set of conditions. He assumed that demand was a point of town located in the middle of a supply area with uniform characteristics of relief, fertility, climate and accessibility, etc. and this point remained isolated from the rest of the world. He further assumed that the cost of transport was proportional to the distance. Under these assumptions, Von Thunen discovered that production was located in a series of belts around the town according to the ratio of distance to value of goods produced. The higher the ratio, the closer the location of the production centres to the town. He later relaxed the assumptions and discovered distortion of the belts by differences in transportation and production costs and by additional points of demand. Within the 'isolated state' Von Thunen's model, therefore, considers the relationship of points of demand to the areas of supply and describes this two-sector economy in equilibrium that is the maximization of economic return. However, Von Thunen and many others since his time have been unable to describe the conditions under which the equilibrium state may be reached. The twin facts of knowing the existence of equilibrium in a system or not and recognizing the conditions under which it may exist, throw a great deal of light on the consistency and completeness of the statements of the model.

The interest in the concept of equilibrium in models that stress locational characteristics emerged with the gradual development of the location theory. Von Thunen's equilibrium model, which formed the bases for some of the subsequent locational studies. Weber, in 1907, attempted to determine the existence of laws governing the location of industries. While Von Thunen was interested in the problem of location of areas in space, Weber was concerned with the location of points. He considered three major forces, the differentials in transport costs, labour costs, and the factors of agglomeration of raw materials as the determinants of best location. He was basically concerned with the principles by which costs could be minimized in the choice of optimum location and, therefore, his ideas are better known as the 'least cost' or 'cost minimization' theory. The different industries would have different optimum locations depending upon the nature and volume of inputs and outputs and, hence difference in the cost structures observed. Weber's theory recognises transport and non-transport factors of localized and ubiquitous materials. The end result was to find the optimum location that would maximize profits by minimizing the total cost. This achieves a balance between the minimum cost and the maximum profits, under certain specified conditions. Once this balance is achieved, equilibrium is maintained in Weber's theory. But this equilibrium actually never exists because some analysts have concluded that firms do not attempt to maximize profits at all. Also, Weber's static model does not take into account such factors as changes in the cost of transportation and the use of alternative fuels. The main criticism of Weber's theory is that it determines the location by analyzing the pattern of inputs and does not sufficiently considers the strength and pattern of market areas.

The central theme of the location theory is expressed in a question posed by Christaller: "are there laws which determine the number, size and distribution of cities"? Christaller hypothesized an ordering principle for the size, number and distribution of central places. Given an isotropic plain surface with uniform terrain and resource localization, an uniform distribution of population and purchasing power, and equal transport facilities in all directions, a definite hierarchy of central places would emerge. The central places of each hierarchical level world are uniformly spaced in a hexagonal pattern. Christaller postulated and provided models of three hexagonal hierarchies of central places according to the principles of marketing, transportation and administration. Christaller's most widely known model of the size and distribution of central places are based on the principles of marketing. He suggested that central places are arranged in a hexagonal lattice and each central place is surrounded by a hexagonal market area.

A hexagonal lattice of markets is also the least cost lattice. In other words, money spent on obtaining an article is divided between transportation cost and price of article in the market. Thus the problem of locating a central place is one of minimizing the distance travelled by customers while maximizing the profitability of the activity. This reflects a static equilibrium state of central place system. Since the above isotropic conditions are seldom met, it cannot be expected to find perfect uniformity in central place patterns. However, we can expect a tendency towards the equilibrium state of the system because of the changing socio-economic structure of the society.

Concepts of Urban Regional Development Growth Foci

According to R.P. Misra there are four tiers of the concept of "growth foci" which help in urbanization and regional development in India.

Service Centres of the Local Level

Such centres are urban centres or larger villages of lowest villages of lowest rank in the urban development having a population of 5,000 to 25,000 concentrated at one nucleated settlement or detached into a number of tiny hamlets. The service centres of this category have the functional units of grocery shops, general merchandise shops, minor repair facilities, tailor shops, barber shops, restaurants, primary and middle schools, post-offices, co-operatives, community centres and other necessary infrastructural facilities. Such centres are generally the headquarters of Mukhia or Sarpanch with a few agricultural extension workers of the government.

Growth Points

These form the second high category of service centres in any region. For the sake of regional development growth points play a crucial role. Such growth points will serve at least 10 to 20 smaller service centres. The population of such centres will range from 50,000 to 1,00,000. It is just like a major urban centre of higher market place like Munger.

Growth Centres

In the hierarchy of growth foci the third level centres are called growth centres. Growth centres are necessarily the production centres and manufacturing is the chief function. In this way, it is a centre of marked secondary and tertiary functions. They will serve a population of 1,00,000 to 2,00,000 having a wider zone of influence. Hence, it is just the functional character of such a development node, which is liable to be called growth centres. Thus it is the industrial hub of the area, which it serves. It has also the facility of grain collection, storage godown including fertilizer, pesticide and agri-implements, besides college and technological institutions.

Growth Pole

At highest level of the foci hierarchy lies the growth poles. Such centres may have a population of 5,00,000 to 25,00,000. In growth pole tertiary population has higher share in comparison with secondary and primary services. They are the focal points of the regional economic development having predominance of financial, educational, technological and industrial sectors. In this way the growth pole hypotheses is indispensable for national, regional and local level planning processes.

The Theory of Development Poles

It was first propounded by Francis Perroux but it has got an important place in French regional economy just like the balanced and steady growth theories. The approach of Perroux holds that analysis of sustained growth of total production should concentrate on the process by which various functions appear, grow and decline in temporal dimensions. It also emphasizes that growth rates which vary considerably from one sector to another and entrepreneurial innovation is a dominant factor in explaining the growth process, which takes the form of a succession of dynamic sectors or poles in time. Here regional interest has been aroused in the pole concept by emphasizing that growth is concentrated in various spatial foci as well as in leading industrial functional zone useful in analyzing various consequences of alternative choice of location. According to Perroux "growth does not appear every where at the same time. It shows itself in points or poles with variable intensities. It spreads by different channels and with variable financial effects on the economy as a whole. This did not consider that development pole is equivalent to a key industry, an economic base, an industrial zone, or even some geographically concentrated phenomenon. Rather Perroux interpreted it essentially in the economic and functional sense.

The Concept of Dominance

It first of all appeared in French economic literature and it explains a dynamic interpretation of economic activity. For Perroux the effect of domination "consists of an irreversible process or partially reversible influence exercised by different central places inside the city. An economic unit exercises this effect by reasons of its dimension, its negotiating strength, the nature of its activity or because it belongs to a zone of dominant activity. The effect of domination has both economic and geographic dimensions, abstracted from any consideration of geographic space. Besides, as soon as any inequality among firms appears the branch is opened by which cumulative effect of domination insinuates itself. In terms of geographic space dominant and propulsive industries make the cities in which they are located and poles of their regions.

Conflicting Tendencies in Spatial Development

Hirschman emphasized the spatial concentration of economic activity with in the framework of his theory of unbalanced growth. He argued that development strategies should concentrate on a relatively few sectors rather than on widely dispersed projects. The key sectors would be determined by measuring backward linkage and forward linkage effects in terms of input-output maxima. In such a situation the growth is communicated from the leading sectors of the economy to the followers, from one firm to the other. The advantage of this approach over balanced growth where every activity expends perfectly in step with every other is that it leaves considerable scope to induce investment decisions and economizes over principal scarce resource namely "genuine decision-making". Myrdal's concepts of "back wash and spread" effects involve the workings of population migration, trade and capital movements, he emphasized about the selective nature of migration from the hinter-land to the growth centres, where specially youngsters are more prone to migrate. He considers the higher fertility rate of poor races and their impact on the working age group to total population ratio, whose effects may be unfavourable in the hinterland. Similarly, capital and income flow to growth centres will continue due to induced investment. Myrdal recognized the critical significance of non-economic factors to the cumulative process of maintaining poverty in the hinterland. The inability to support adequate health and education facilities and the conservative outlook, all are detrimental to the experimental and rational orientation of an economically well off society. The spread effects are meant for increased outlets of the hinterland agricultural products and tendency for technical advance to diffuse from the growth centre. The spread effects will be stronger at the higher level of economic development. The attractiveness of a growth centre is also weakened by using external technological diseconomies and higher labour costs. Ultimately the national and central governments are also likely to initiate policies directed towards greater regional equality.

Friedman's Core-Periphery Model

This model was initially put forward in a study of Venezuelan regional development policy by Friedman. He felt that development is the unfolding of creativeness in a society through a successive series of structural transformation by the process of innovation. Development taken place from small number of "centre of change" located at the points of highest potential interaction within a communication field (Fig. 5.2).

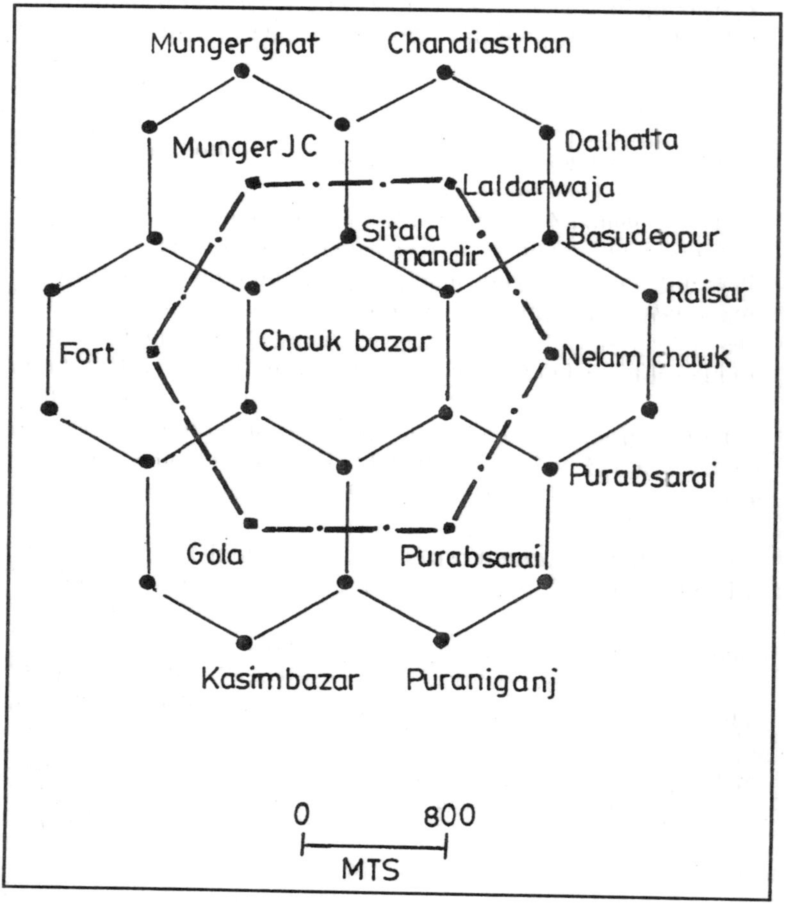

Fig. 5.2 : Model of Central Place Hierachy in Munger

Innovations diffuse from these centres to areas of lower potential interaction. Such "core regions" are major centres of innovation change, while all other territory consists of "peripheral regions" which are dependent on core regions for development. It has been controlled by the following processes of feedback effects of core regions growth.

(a) The weakening of the periphery by resource transfer to the core;
(b) Increased interaction and innovation in the core;
(c) A high rate of innovation due to higher expectations and lower risks;
(d) The modernization effect;
(e) Social and institutional change favouring innovation;
(f) Linkage effects or the tendency of innovations to induce at another innovations; and
(g) Production effects which increase scale and agglomeration of economics.

In India State capitals may be known as core regions within a nested hierarchy of spatial systems. The peripheral regions are dependent on core regions by virtue of supply and consumer relations, including administrative organization.

Lasuen Growth Poles and Organizational Space

The growth centre concept has immensely helped in studying the problems of regional development through industrial organization. Lasuen believes that the "diffusion channels of specific information will become less and less selective and the spread of adoptions more extensive over sectoral and geographic space, and economic development faster and less polarized". He proposes two-faced strategy to avoid problems of regional economic disparities. At this stage, it is required to create a stronger interaction between all points across all topological spaces. This can be achieved by consolidating all plants into large multi-plant, multi-product, multicity of firms by fostering inter-firms linkages. These should also be a very flexible policy to increase the relative attractiveness of lagging regions. Capital, credit, training, service, infrastructure and other firms of assistance to public and private firms should take account of the different priorities of firms at various stages of organization in case they are to be effective.

Dynamic Model of the Growth of Town

In the beginning of such town had taken place during ancient period in the forest environment, when there were no transport routes at all. Later on, with the beginning of second settlement in the neighbourhood might have given rise to one way connection of transport linkage. This may be known as K=1. Further, in addition to the directional connection of transport routes as K=2. Similarly three centres give three directional linkages as K=3, four directions as K=4, five directions as K=5, and six directions as K=6 for the densest packing of centres of the same order (Fig. 5.3).

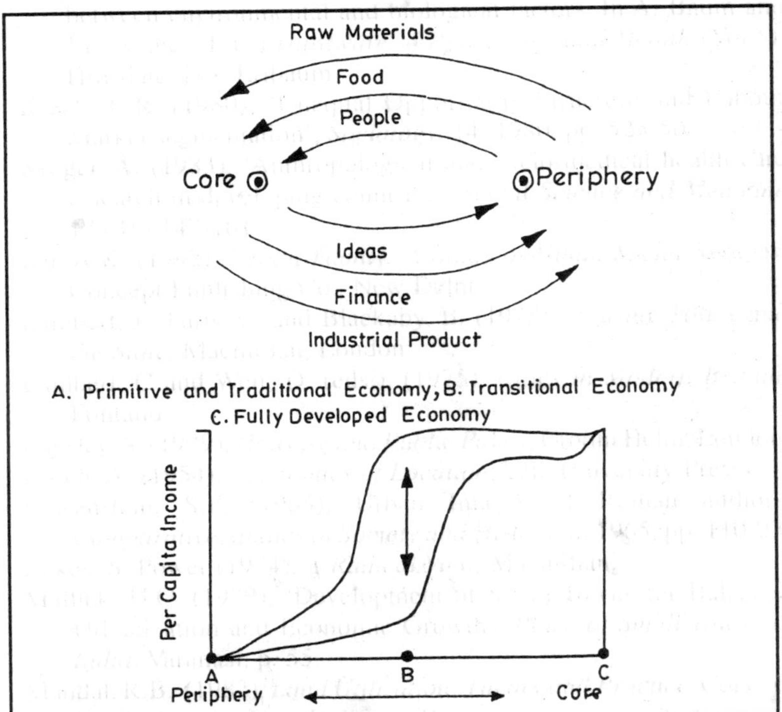

Fig. 5.3 : Core Periphery Model and the Process of Feedback Mechanism

But with the increase in number of centres in a triangle or in a hexagon, the K value may increase upto a very high figure. This will help in finding out the problem areas for infrastructural planning of services in relation to the location of first ranking market centres of Bhagalpur in the study area. This model also believes in the hierarchy of market centres according to the increasing *K* value for a particular point in an equilateral triangle. This may be analysed with the number of transport route connections in between Munger and Bhagalpur cities and the villages of the surrounding region. This will automatically give high *K* value for the centres treated as intracity central place hierarchy. In this way, the model also satisfies the conditions of hierarchy of urban centres, keeping in view the consumers of different rural settlements, who visit the cities of Munger and Bhagalpur.

Conclusion

As we perceived about the location of cities, it includes the site and situation on which the town stands and the importance of the town in relation to the places of surrounding area. The concepts are wholly relying on the spatial distribution of cities in relation to situations of the area and the surrounding villages in the hinterland.

In locational decisions wetland measures have to be considered so that more and more benefit could be occurred out of the locational decision. In the cities Von Thumen's model is best fit, which considered the location of market and crops in different sectors around the market centre. As the distance increases from the central part of the town, the inferior crops coming to compete each other. Near the market centre important crops are located which need more attention or protection.

REFERENCES

Achuta Rao, T.N. (1967), The Concept of Twin Cities, *Geographical Review of India*, Vol. 29, pp.104-107.

Ahmad, E. (1956), Origin and Evolution of Town of the Uttar Pradesh; *Geographical Outlook*, Vol. 1, pp. 38-58.

Ahmad, S. (1950), *Dacca; A Study in Urban History and Development*, Curzon Press, London.

Anal, S.K. Singh (1980), *Origin and Growth of Cities*, Concept Publishing Co., New Delhi.

Berry, B.J.L. (1968), Theories of Urban Location'. *Annals of the Association of American Geographers*, Resource Paper I, Washington.

Buckley, W. (1967), *Sociology and Modern System Theory*, Englewood Cliffs, New Jersey, Prentice Hall.

Christaller, W. (1966), *Central Places in Southern Germany*, Prentice Hall, New Jersey, p. 64.

Ellefesen, R.A. (1962), 'City Hinterland Relationship in India', in *India's Urban Future,* Oxford University Press, Bombay.

Friedman (1966), "Two Concepts of Urbanization: A Comment", *Urban Affairs Quarterly*, 1, p. 80.

Grimm, F. (1979), *The Settlement System of the GDR*', Leipzig.

Mandal, R.B. (1982), *Land Utilization: Theory and Practice*, Concept Publishing Co., New Delhi, p. 76.

Nath, V. (1962), 'The Village and the Community', in *India's Urban Future* Edited by Roy Turner, University of California Press, pp.151-153.

Weber, M.J. (1969), "Sub-optional Behaviour and the Concept of Maximum Profits in Location Theory", *Australian Geographical Studies*, 7, p. 1 .

6 MEASUREMENT OF THE LEVELS OF QUALITY OF LIFE

Most of the migrants to the cities of Munger and Bhagalpur come from rural areas who get attracted due to descent living but the problem of unemployment forced them to be landless, homeless, jobless and without any financial means to occupy the residential houses legally. Hence, the poor people have been forced to constructs their houses on vacant land and they live as illegal occupants of the city. This type of squatting creates conflict with those who are law abiding citizens which leads conflict with those who are abiding citizens which leads to violence and hence, such people are really a burden on urban life.

The quality of life of people in urban areas depends on activities like trade and commerce, cultural and religious events, recreational housing and transport infrastructure available to the urban residents. It has been felt that infant mortality and life expectancy of urban people are good indicators of the prevailing quality of life of people.

For the urban people of Munger and Bhagalpur the basic needs identified are shelter, availability of food grains, water supply, health care and the methods of sewage disposal.

The availability of bi-cycles, motorcycles, scooters, cars, black and white televisions, colour televisions, lighting arrangement with animals and without animals in the house, climatic condition, dress material, food and drinking habits count much in the quality of life of urban people. It has also been decided by the presence of wife or no wife, with a disease or no disease, vegetarian or non-vegetarian, service latrine or safety latrine, close to the temple or no temple, close to the grocery shop or no grocery shop, a literate person or an illiterate person, musical taste to no musical taste, hail and hearty or timid personality and so on.

Wider road or narrow hooked and crooked road, *pucca* houses or *kucha* houses caste affiliation, income potential, sense of leadership all count much in judging the quality of life. Employment creates socio-economic resource whereas unemployment brings inequality in the labour market. These are the embarrassing situations to judge the quality of life of a person, as he or she is not in a position to maintain a consistently stable system of living in urban areas. It has in need of some urgent planning so that squatting people could take a shy of relief.

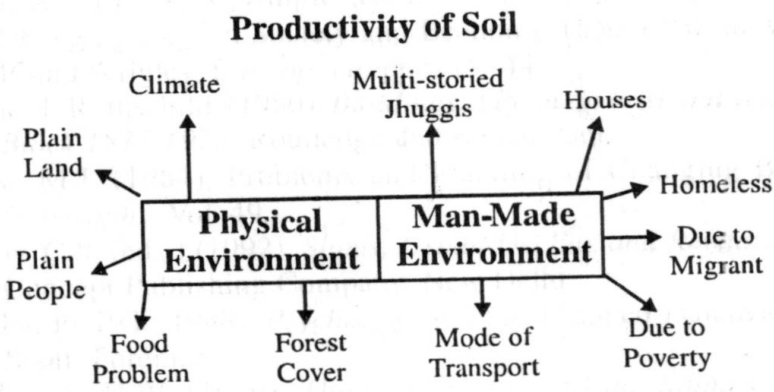

FACTORS AFFECTING URBAN LIFE

General People Life

The main roads in the cities of Munger and Bhagalpur are metalled. The municipality maintains about 165 kilometres of *pucca* roads within

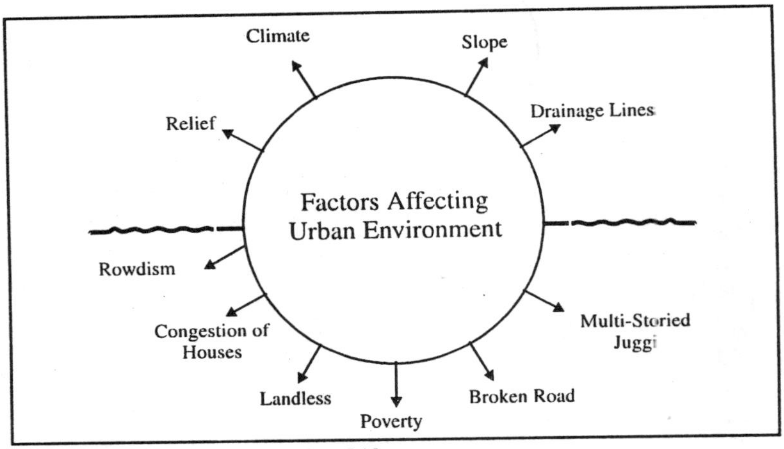

Fig. 6.1 : Factors Affecting Urban Life

the city. The vehicles within the city are buses, rickshaws, cycles, tamtams and bullock carts. There are private cars and taxis also.

The cities of Munger and Bhagalpur have one dak bungalow, two inspection bungalows and several *dharamshalas*. There are some cheap roadside eating houses, tea stalls and a few hotels of poor standard for temporary accommodation.

Being the headquarters of the district a large number of government offices are located here. They include the offices of the Commissioner, the Collector, Sub-divisional Officer, Public Works Department, Assistant Registrar, Co-operative Societies, District and Sub-divisional Agricultural Officer, Project Executive Officer, Superintendent of Police and the Superintendent of Central Jail, etc. The Bhagalpur town has the office of T.M. Bhagalpur University located in Lalbag campus.

The cities have the junior basic schools, 50 primary schools including two for girls, one middle school for girls, three higher secondary schools, including one for girls with 1,010 students and 49 teachers and 12 colleges each with about 1400 students and 45 professors and lecturers.

Besides, the cities have one senior residential school with about 50 students and twelve teachers each. The students are provided free lodging and boarding. There is one medical attendant to look after the health of the students. The entire expenditure is borne by the State Government. The residential school at Munger and Bhagalpur gets Rs.78,282 annually. In order to solve the problems of accommodation of students of the Scheduled Castes and Scheduled Tribes, the State Government has started welfare hostels in the city which accommodate 150 students in each town.

The cities of Munger and Bhagalpur have four libraries each. On an average about 65 persons visit each of the libraries daily. The cities have one town club where indoor games are played and four parks for the children, one managed by the municipality and one by the Irrigation Department.

In the cities of Munger and Bhagalpur residential areas are the largest component of the built-up space. It consists of various types of houses, arranged along streets of weird design. Changes in the built up area have caused a number of problems in the physical fabric of residential areas. Fast increase in population has resulted in an acute shortage of residential accommodation and overcrowding, particularly in the Bhagalpur town.

The residential areas, in Munger and Bhagalpur are characterized by very poor sanitary conditions with open gutters, choked water refuge drains with sullage and quite often found on both sides of the street. Recent growth of squatter settlements in the cities of Munger and Bhagalpur provides instances of extreme congestion, overcrowding and insanitary living.

Quality of Life in Commercial Areas

The main shopping areas of Munger and Bhagalpur are located along the main road of fort to Purabsarai and Champanala to Zero respectively. They form the focal point of commercial activities and is, sometimes known as ' Gudari Bazar' or 'Gola Bazar' where retail establishments for general stores dealing in convenience goods cater the needs of city population. There is a considerable variation in the intensity and distributional pattern of commercial nucleation, including extreme congestion and overcrowding of shopping units noted on the sides of main road of the city and in the Gola Market. The pattern of shopping is always old-styled and appalling congestion prevails on the roadside and pavement as well. Some shopping areas are found in narrow and winding lanes where congestion and overcrowding have become too glaring phenomena. In fact, inhabitants in the commercial core are confronted with health hazards due to congestion and overcrowding.

The location of 'Gudari Bazar' in the central business areas presents special problems. Footpath vendors selling fruits and vegetables, meat and fish etc. obstruct the smooth flow of traffic, both vehicular and pedestrian. Some shops display their salable goods on the pavement which also aggravate the problems of congestion. The restaurants of roadside and tea-stalls in the commercial areas throw their refuge of the kitchen on the pavements, making the area more filthier and dirtier.

Problems of People's Life in the Industrial Area

Industrial establishments and workshops also add to the complexity of problems in the cities of Munger and Bhagalpur. It has been noted that small industrial establishments generally occur in residential areas inhabited by working class people. For example, in Bhagalpur silk mill is located in the residential area along the station road. Flour and oil mills also occupy similar locations. Small industries including metal works, saw mills and furniture making, often occur in residential and commercial segments. This creates host of problems including the nuisance of noise due to taping of metal-beaters or black-smiths, grinding and vibration of flour milling and foul odours of the soap and leather factories. The problems of noise, dust and chemical pollutions prevail in most parts of the cities of Munger and Bhagalpur. Bullock-carts and hand-driven *thellas* are also create transport bottlenecks or congestion. It has been felt that pedestrian movement is sluggish and hazardous especially during the evening hours in the cities.

Problems of Educational Institutions

With the field observation the cities of Munger and Bhagalpur reveal an uneven distribution of educational institutions. Though the government has taken over the management of primary and secondary schools but there is still a lot of variations in the amenities available in public, private and missionary schools. Keeping in view, the large size of student population, the number of nursery, primary, middle and high schools are insufficient. Some of these schools are located in noisy, overcrowded and unhygienic conditions prevailing on the main road area or the heart of the town. Consequently, these schools cannot provide the basic needs like playground and lawns. Though the colleges and technical institutes are catering to the needs of higher education, which are situated on periphery of the cities, but they still lack in facilities like well-equipped laboratories, libraries, hostels and playgrounds.

Lack of Proper Medical Facilities

Though the cities of Munger and Bhagalpur have the facilities of hospitals and dispensaries but the facilities of hospitals and dispensaries available are quite inadequate. Consequently, large number of city dwellers are deprived of the medical aids. The endemic nature of malaria and other tropical diseases in Bhagalpur calls for special preventive and curative measures.

Problems of Parks and Recreational Areas

The city dwellers of Munger and Bhagalpur are in need of recreational facilities to relieve the drudgery of urban living. People can breathe fresh air in parks and playgrounds. Other recreational facilities like cinema, theatre, club and picnic spots, help to re-invigorate the town dwellers. The cities of Munger and Bhagalpur provide these facilities in a limited quantity only. However, Bhagalpur has large open spaces under orchards, ponds and vegetable gardens. Playgrounds attached to colleges and schools are located on the periphery of the city only. The general public is not supposed to make use of them. Most of these playgrounds and parks are poorly maintained and used badly.

Traffic and Transportation Problems

From traffic point of view, the arrangement and layout of roads, their relative position and means of inter-communication are matters of fundamental importance. The cities of Munger and Bhagalpur have narrow roads which are incapable of bearing heavy traffic. In the cities of Munger and Bhagalpur there is no good quality of road which could be considered suitable for bearing heavy urban traffic. The condition of road is far from satisfactory. Several roads are unmetalled and without good pavements for pedestrian traffic, which create congestion and traffic hazards.

Planning for Improvement of Residential Areas

Residential area happens to be the largest component of the urban life of Munger and Bhagalpur. Here, the problems of obsolete dwellings, congestions, overcrowding and in sanitary conditions require urgent consideration. In the cities of Munger and Bhagalpur less land pre-dwelling has become and essential ingredient of town planning, both in physical and structural terms. A sound development planning has been required to improve the living conditions in these cities by providing ample facilities for better roads and other civic amenities.

Thus following measures may be suggested for the improvement of residential areas in Munger and Bhagalpur.

1. First of all, haphazard construction of dwellings in various sections of the town should be stopped through proper municipal legislation. Obsolete and dilapidated buildings, occurring mostly in the older parts of the town, have to be demolished and modern buildings should be constructed on

that place by providing financial assistance at a reasonable rate of interest to the house owners.

2. Bihar Urban Ceiling Act of 1961 should be implemented without any further delay. So that the surplus urban land could be acquired for the development of residential complexes, particularly for the poor people in the middle and lower income groups. The layout plan, allocation of plots and approval of building plans have to be made by the town development authority, which could also supply building materials at approved rates.
3. Formation of town planning unit is suggested so that is could assist the Municipality and N.A.C. in town development. At present Munger and Bhagalpur have no improvement trust or any other town-planning organization.
4. As Munger lines in the seismic zone of India, hence the vertical expansion of buildings has to be restricted, preferably beyond two stories only.
5. Low-lying marshy and wastelands, lying in the urban areas should be reclaimed for developed of residential colonies and other uses. In doing so, due consideration has to be given to the economy of space, provision of public utility services and the expenditure involved.
6. The slum areas in Munger and Bhagalpur need immediate attention. It has been proposed that the slum-dwellers, at present residing under unhygienic conditions in the densely populated parts may be rehabilitated at alternative sites on the outskirts of the town and the slum-cleared areas can be developed into parks and playground.

Suggetions for the Improvement of Commercial Areas

The recent population explosion and increase in the size of Munger and Bhagalpur have resulted in the phenomenal growth of commercial activities. This has caused an overlap of functional uses in these cities. Hence, to relieve congestion and overcrowding in the C.B.A. a proposal is made to shift the residences to other areas and the space vacated may be renovated into shops, showrooms and other commercial establishments. This could be done by persuasion, legislation and provision for financial assistance. The 'Gudari Bazar', located in the heart of the town, needs also to be moved to some other convenient location so as to ease congestion. The space so vacated can then be allotted for retail business on hire-purchase basis. Thus, the wholesale and retail trade may function at separate locations. Big godowns and warehouses may be established either in close proximity to the railway station or at entry points of important roads into the town or, wherever ample open space is available. This may provide cheap and convenient storage facilities for bulky goods, like, jute, and other agricultural produce. Thus, the congestion in the central business areas where some of the warehouses are at present locate should be relieved. Pavement shops need not to function in the commercial core of the town and all encroachments on road to be stopped.

Provision for a municipal market, selling general merchandise and perishable goods, has to be made in each ward. This will also contribute to the easing of congestion in the central business area. Paved foot-ways for pedestrian traffic have to be constructed in the commercial areas. This will increase street capacity. The provision for bypass roads has to be made so that intertown traffic need not touch intermediate stations. There is also need for developing suburban markets to cater to the needs of expanding town.

Conclusion

The cities of Munger and Bhagalpur in the State of Bihar have been confronted with a large number of problems due to its unprecedented growth in different directions and dimensions. This has resulted in overcrowding, congestion, poor housing facilities, encroachments on open spaces and roadside, abnormal influx of rural population in different sectors of urban area and rise of shopping units due to unemployment.

In order to bring modernity in the urban centres of Munger and Bhagalpur, it is an important task for social scientists and economists not adequately realized up till now. The plan document of Munger and Bhagalpur city plan does not contain any reference to the positive characteristics of urban economic development, and the dynamics by which it could develop. At last we could say that increase in urbanization should be treated as a positive factor in bringing modernity as well as economic development.

REFERENCES

Abrams, C. (1953), Urban Land Problems and Policies; *Housing Town and Country Planning Bulletin* 7, UNO.

Beckinsale, R.P. and Houseton, J.M. (1968), *Urbanization and Its Problems,* Blackwell.

Bhat, L.S. *et al.* (1976), *Micro Level Planning*, K.B. Publications, New Delhi.

Bruse, G. and Whitemen, D.F. (1953), *An Approach to Urban Planning*, Princeton University Press.

Gandhi, Indira (1975), Haphazard Growth of Our Cities, *Yojana,* Vol. XIX No. 15, November, pp. 5-8.

Hoselitz, B.F. (1959), Cities of India and Their Problems; *Annals of the Association of American Geographers*, Vol. 49, pp. 223-231.

Wise, M.J. (1964), *Problems and Planning of Changing Britain Geography,* Vol. 49.

7 SLUMS AND SQUATTERS FOUND IN THE URBAN AREAS

The intensity of slum is very high in Munger and Bhagalpur because the sitting condition is absolutely insanitary. The heap of garbage lies here and there and the living conditions of the poor menials and the labour class people are absolutely unfit for human living. Moreover, with the decline of service facilities and increase of population the slums are cropping up everywhere in the town.

These days slums have created a panic for city development. It has been a serious issue for the town planning bodies not only in India but in Europe and North America as well. Slums are the marginal areas of cities where the service facilities are poor, people are illiterate, drinking water supply is miserably on lowest ebb and the vice of under-worlds predominate the scene. The study of slum is meaningful for environmental modification and ameliorating the problems of urban areas for providing more amenities to the ailing masses. This type of study finds ground mostly in European countries, where the town centres are the problem areas for city dwellers and people want clean air to breath. In such a situation, this study has been directly related to highlight the urban problems in a developing urban scenario of Munger and Bhagalpur.

Now-a-days, the city fathers have taken less care for cleaning different wards and this has resulted into the growth of slums such as Heru diara, Dilawarpur, Topkhana Bazar, Guhiapokher, Dalhatta, Murgiachak, Ghositola, Kashim Bazar and Puraniganj in Munger and Sahibganj, Champanagar in Bhagalpur.

Problems Studied

Slums and Squatters have been considered as the lopsided development of urban centres in the Third World countries. They are illegally occupied houses and creating a menace of environmental pollution and degradation of urban living conditions. These areas are not at all considered as settlements to stay in our urban society because slums and squatters provide a milieu of negligence of social order, economic backwardness, drudgery of leading happy life besides political indifference. Slums are the dirty urban areas where the drains are full of mud and dirty water of the houses, full of filth and flies, mosquitoes and insects abound. The roads are either unmetalled or full of potholes where even passersby have to wade through the muddy water and creating a sense of danger in walking even in day time, what to talk of night. The slums have mostly no road-lights, latrines are service, the road corners are full of garbage and the pigs abound. Hen and varieties of livestock wealth are creating a sense of fear to walk for a sensible person. Most of the houses are occupied illegally without land ownership and houses have been constructed without obtaining legal permission from the municipal authority.

This chapter has been designed to undertake the upgradation of slums and squatter settlements in the cities of Munger and Bhagalpur with a view to highlight the socio-economic life of the urban society in terms of environmental pollution which has been developing sense of insecurity in urban areas not only for the urban authorities but also for the planners, administrators and society in general.

Both Munger and Bhagalpur have developed as administrative, industrial and religious centres and hence these two urban centres favour the concentration of the unemployed, religious-minded and unwanted people from the rural areas who are problematic to the urban society and developing as a short of fungus in the form of refugee as there is no law to put restrictions for these people to live as refugees in common places of urban land. Hence, the problem of this chapter is to highlight these issues besides suggesting measures for their uplift not on the bases of social, economic and humanitarian grounds for social justice and giving a home for the homeless.

Justification of Study

This study has been undertaken on social and humanitarian grounds for the emancipation of the people from economic ills and slavery in the urban society. Such an insanitary condition and polluted environment which are found near squatter settlements and in slum areas should not be tolerated at any cost because the problems of one person in the society is the problem of all others who are living in the nearby areas. From the point of view of sociology, geography and urban economics this topic should be in the forefront of research from the academic point of view besides the welfare of human society.

Theoretical Principles Involved

The concept of feedback mechanism demarcates the seen of Gunnar Myrdal's cumulative causation because poverty is the cause of greater poverty, insanitation is the cause of greater insanitation. On such a basis of social order and quality of life the people living in squatter settlements and slum areas have been forced or divorced by the society to live in such an environmental condition. Hence, they are landless, insane, illiterate, unhealthy, illclothed, and for these facts they suffer from diseases and the vices of underworlds. All these are points, which will be considered in theoretical formulation of a plan for the upgradation of slums and squatter settlements in the urban centres of Munger and Bhagalpur

Characteristics of Slum Residents

(a) The families living in slum and squatter settlements are mostly middle class and poor.
(b) Most of the squatting people are landless labourers.
(c) Slum dwellers mostly live in areas of low land value due to their low income.
(d) People living in squatter areas are biased with illegal profession in most of the cases.
(e) People living in squatter areas are some time suffer from serious diseases and hence they are divorced from the original home. They mostly indulge in unsocial behaviour, vices of underworlds and other related problems.

Approaches

The Government of India with special reference to Kolkata conurbation has given planned housing colonies in order to solve the problems of Bustees in Kolkata. This is a glorious example in the world which have given impetus for the other Government to think positively about the problem, so that people living in slum and squatter settlements may be given the facilities of drinking water, a permanent site for home, health facilities, primary education for the children besides access up to roads and work places. Keeping in view of this West Germany has organized an International symposia on the up gradation of slums and squatter settlements in Berlin on 15th of November 1986. The emphasis was mostly on field survey, spatial arrangement, design formulation and inform the people and the Government about seriousness of the problems. As this study is more close to the urban quality of life and regional analysis may be preferred for appreciating the problems in different areas of the cities of Munger and Bhagalpur.

Methodology

For understanding the types and patterns of slum and their growth the basic data collected through fieldwork in the cities of Munger and Bhagalpur and analysis have been made. The history of each slum and their characteristic patterns have been made through library work in the municipality and personal interview with knowledgeable persons within the municipal boundary. The intensity of slum have been analysed with the help of quality of life found in the area.

Sources of Data

For slum study, the map of different wards have been collected from the Munger and Bhagalpur municipalities and other figures collected from fieldwork. The data relates to the number of houses, occupational structure of people. Literacy and living conditions of slum-dwellers who are engaged in different jobs in the urban area.

Slums of Bhagalpur Town

Bhagalpur city is one of the important places of Eastern Bihar, famous for silk, can be divided into 37 wards for administrative purposes. It was the capital of Anga region during ancient period and now the administration centre of Bhagalpur Division.

The total area of Bhagalpur city is 30.17 sq. km, situated between 25°10′20″ to 25°17′45″ N latitudes and between 86°55′30″ to 87°1′15″ eastern longitudes.

The ancient capital of Raja Karn and famous silk city of India. Bhagalpur is situated on the southern bank of holy river Ganga. Now it is a famous city and education centre of Eastern Bihar.

Although there are 37 wards in Bhagalpur but the Municipality Administration has declared twenty-five wards as slum area.

Patterns of Slums and Squatter Settlements

In the cities of Munger and Bhagalpur about 45 per cent people are living in slums and squatter settlements. About 60,000 people are living in village centred areas of the city such as Topkhana Bazar, Dilawarpur, Sadipur, Murgiachak, Kasim Bazar, Garden Bazar, Guljarpokhar, Chuabagh, Sandalpur and Chhoti-Kelabari. In all these slum areas one can see heaps of garbage on the road, drains choked with sewage, a huge crowd on the water taps for drinking water, service latrine with daily service, lack of windows in the houses, high occupancy rate, retouched condition of houses besides polluted environment in most of the residential areas (Fig. 7.1).

The main cause for such a pitiable condition is due to the small expanse of the original city centre, but how the addition of new villages into the old city centre have developed in the form of slum due to their unmetalled narrow lanes with potholes at places. All such areas have been included in this way in the cities of Munger and Bhagalpur, a points of slum in these cities. According to 1961 census the following villages are included in the municipal area of the city of Munger, Amarpur, Hasanganj, Adampur, Gauripur, Ayodhya, Shankarpur, Hasanpur, Muzaffarpur, Bag Naulakha and Heru Diara.

In 1971 the following new markets have been added to the old markets of the city and now most of them have developed as slums of incurable in nature because the material conditions getting worse

Table 7.1 : Conditions of Squatter Settlements in the Munger City (2004)

Squatter Areas	*No. of Houses*	*Dominant Caste*
1. Purabsarai	42	Manjhi
2. Laldarwaja	31	Dome
3. Laldarwajaghat	25	Dome
4. No. Two Gumti	33	Halkhor
5. Fort Areas	25	Nat
6. Near Police Line	21	Manjhi
7. Heru Diara	62	Yadava, Muslim
8. Sudurkhana	30	Gareri
9. No. Five Gumti	28	Muslim
10. North of Refujee Colony	50	Bengali

Source : Collected through fieldwork by the author July, 2004.

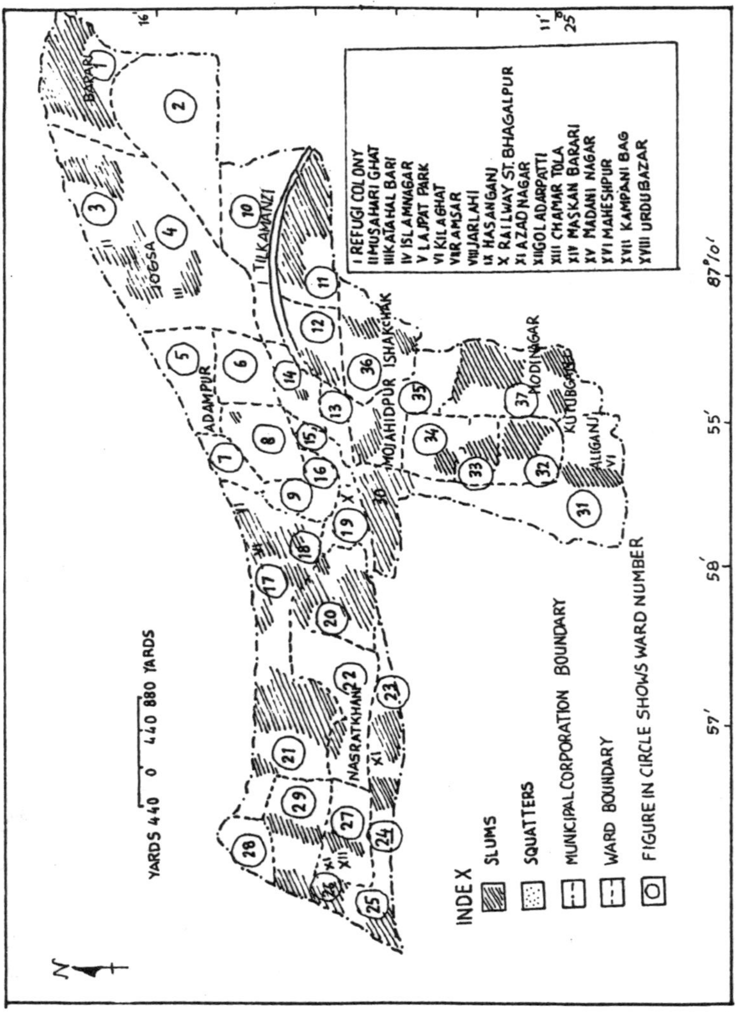

Fig. 7.1 : Bhagalpur City : Distribution of Slums and Squatters 2005

day by day. They are: Kasim Bazar, Safiasarai, Purabsarai, Laldarwaja, Murgiachak, Neelam cinema, Bekapur, Pasratapatti, Lohapatti, Babua Bazar and Gola.

This shows that the transformation of villages into urban centres is a continuous process and this has helped in the expansion of the urban boundary in the form of slum-infested areas.

In the cities of Munger and Bhagalpur the squatter settlements are found in the following places:

It has been found that people living in squatter areas serve the cities of Munger and Bhagalpur as labourers, rickshaw pullers, beggars, pick-pocketers, child lifters, shoe makers, besides waste glass, scrap iron and paper collectors (Fig.7.2).

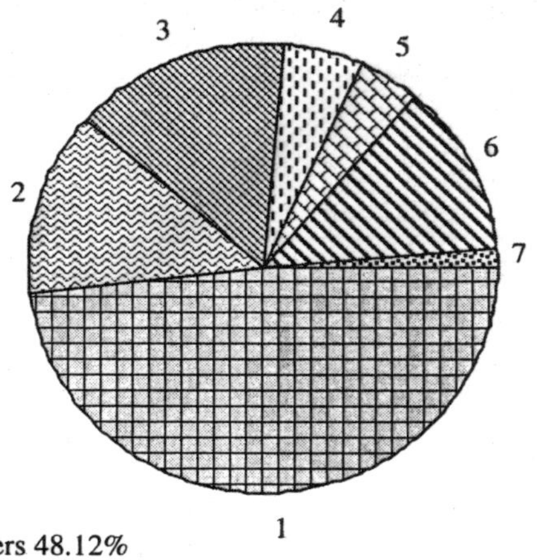

Fig. 7.2 : Occupational Structure of People Living in Slum Area of Purabsarai, Munger

Regarding the permanent settlements of these inhabitats living in squatters is that they don't want to get uprooted from the place where they are living. This is because they have their zone of influence from which they are getting their livelihood. The second point is that some of them are living in a restricted area where in no case they can be settled. So far as their housing condition is concerned two roomed simple houses along with the facility of water and safety latrine should be an essential component, because the present condition is so miserable that no sane people can think about such a living. The sitting condition for such a settlement may be double row houses along the roadside so that they can clean them easily. There will be no problem of constructing fresh roads so that they may be very close to the society for their necessities of life.

The slums and squatter people of Purabsarai, Munger are mostly labour class people besides Municipal workers, rickshaw pullers, beggars, vendors and *fakirs*. Most of them came from Lakshmipur, Sakarpur, Tarapur, Sangrampur, Chilla, Bela, Belhar, Chandpur and Akbarnagar. These places are located in south eastern part of the district of Munger where these people have been harassed by Yadava's of the area which act as a push force and the opportunity of getting a good job in the cities of Munger and Bhagalpur is a pull force for attracting these people.

Table 7.2 : Slums and Squatter Residents of Purabsarai (2004)

Occupation of Residents	*No. of families*	*Male*	*Female*	*Place of origin*
Labourers	18	42	35	Laksmipur, Sakarpur, Tarapur, Sangrampur, Chilha.
Municipal Workers	5	10	11	Bela, Tarapur
Rikshwapuller	6	11	13	Belhar, Sangrampur Chandpur.
J.R.S. College Male	3	3	6	Sangrampur
Beggar	4	4	4	Laksmipur
Glass, Paper, Tin Collector	5	10	10	Bilhar Sangrampur
Fakir	1	1	1	Akbarnagar

Conclusions

Slums are the problematic areas in the cities of Munger and Bhagalpur which shows their poverty and lack of facilities given to the public by the planning bodies. It warrants the local government for urgent solution to unemployment problem besides the planned arrangement of residential houses for those who are homeless. Squatting on public land is a crime on the part of the individual whereas slum condition are crime on the part of municipal organization because these cancerous developments could not be tolerated for the proper development of urban society.

REFERENCES

Dickenson, J.P. *et al.* (1983), *A Geography of the Third World;* Methuen, London, pp. 189-91.

Ward, P.M. (1976), 'Intra-City Migration to Squatter Settlements in Mexico City', *Geoforum*, Vol. 5, pp. 369-82.

Ward, P.M., 'The Squatter Settlements as Slum or Housing Solution: Evidence from Mixico City'; *Land Economics*, Vol. 52, No.3, pp. 330-46.

Ulack, R. (1978), "The Role of Urban Squatter Settlement", *Annals of the Association of American Geographers*, Vol. 68, pp. 535-550.

8 SLUMS OF MUNGER AND BHAGALPUR

The people of slum grow up and die in streets of slum. The most wretched among the slum dwellers in Munger live on the wayside pavements of Munger Ghat. They are mainly beggars, rag pickers and rickshaw-pullers (Fig. 8.1).

Some of them have built their shacks but the majority live without any roof. Though several times their shacks have been demolished and the dwellers have been driven out of the boundaries of the Fort by the local administration. They, in absence of any permanent place to live in comeback and rebuild their houses on the same old site.

Nestling in the lap of the Munger Fort and the Brown Sahib's Munger Club, these slum dwellers are most forgotten people who always live in tatters with hunger and despondency attached on their faces. They are born by the wayside, grow up in streets and finally meet their graves in a similar fashion.

But in summer, winter or rainy season, it is they who bear the burnt of the weather God. At night, when the world sleeps affluent people are co-conned in their air-conditioned rooms, the slum dwellers wait for the Sun to arrive braving the vagaries of nature, stray dogs, the *goondas*, the police and the raptiles.

"Bahuji it is not the pump and splendour of the town life that has attracted us," said a slum dweller, a rickshaw-puller, who had come to Munger from Muzaffarpur a decade ago with his wife and there kids, and added, "we still want to live in our village, we have not lost affinity to the village life which is far from the maddening crowded, the din and bustle of the city life. But it is due to the land owning people who in nexus with police and criminals people who in nexus with police and criminals are out to expoit us, make us to work on their land without giving minimum wages, keep us as bounded labourers and literally starve us. It is because of these factors that we have come to the city. Besides, we are also not assured of work round the year in the villages." "But the situation is no better here rather it is worse," said Shakil Ahmad, rag picker, whose father died while he

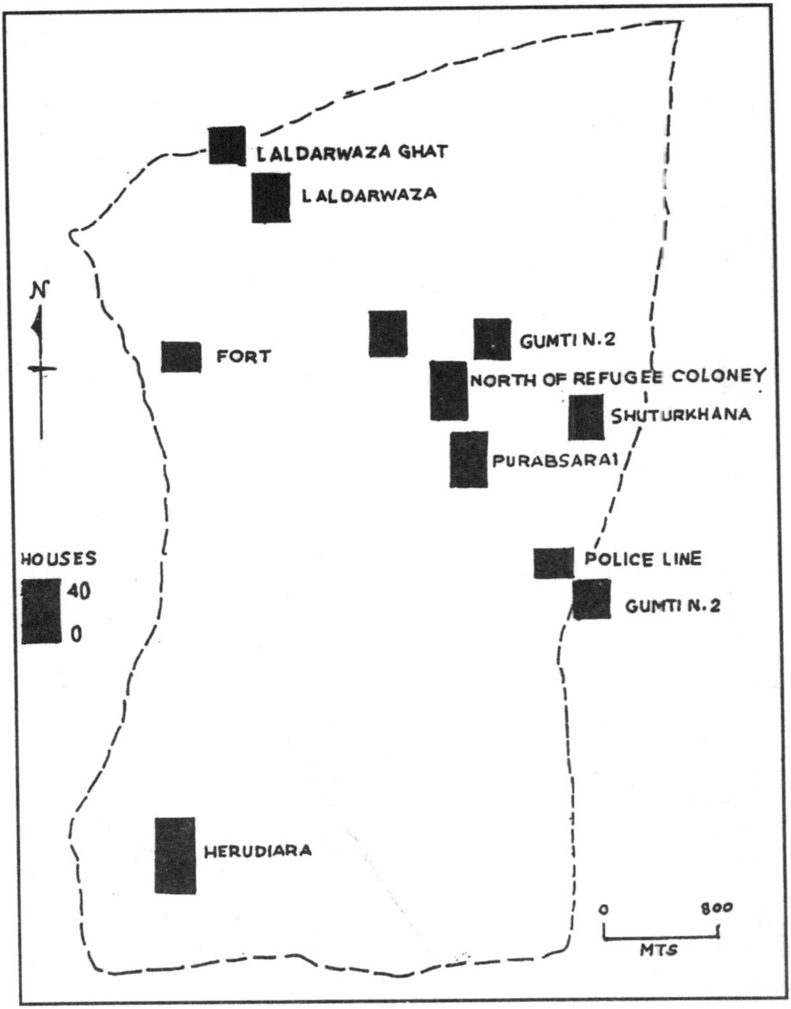

Fig. 8.1 : Patterns of Slums and Squatter Settlements in the City of Munger

was a small kid and since then he has been sustaining his ailing mother and his three younger sisters. He said, "In villages at least there is no ban on drinking water but here we have been denied this." For the dwellers in Munger food is something they have learnt to live without and expect to keep the system joining. Most of them are half-dead breathing skeletons.

According to a social activist, these dwellers are suffering from all kind of ailments like fever, cholera, dysentery and respiratory problems but as they are considered as pariah and a slum on the society, they are denied any medical facility.

He said, "the municipal corporation, the urban development department and the State Government should be blamed for our condition, besides, the society and the people should change their attitude towards the slum and the pavement dwellers."

He said, "Though these provides essential services to the cities, yet they are unwanted. They have been simply reduced to vote banks of the politicians."

Laldarwaja Slum Study

Laldarwaja *mohalla* comes under ward No. 3 of the city of Munger. This study has been done with the help of field investigation on 8-9-2005. This area is bounded by the Ganges diara in the north, Chhotikelawari and Subhas Nagar in the south, Munger junction in the west and outfall drain of Laldarwaja in the east (Fig. 8.2).

Refuge Water Drain

In the eastern part of Laldarwaja there is 10 feet wide and 10 feet deep Nala through which the used water of *mohalla* flows towards the east and ultimately falls into the Ganges, east of Chandiasthan. Another Nala in the form of lowlying area is found along northern flank of Railway line, which runs from Munger Junction up to Gumti No. 2. Another smaller drain passes through a different lane; most of them are open and so dirty that foul smell is coming out of it and full of insects and pests.

Service Latrines

Throughout Laldarwaja *mohalla* mixed type of latrine is found. Only in a few cases, septic latrines are found where as in most other service latrine is found. No one cares to convert it into septic because the residents are poor and the municipal authority demands bribe to grant money for the purpose.

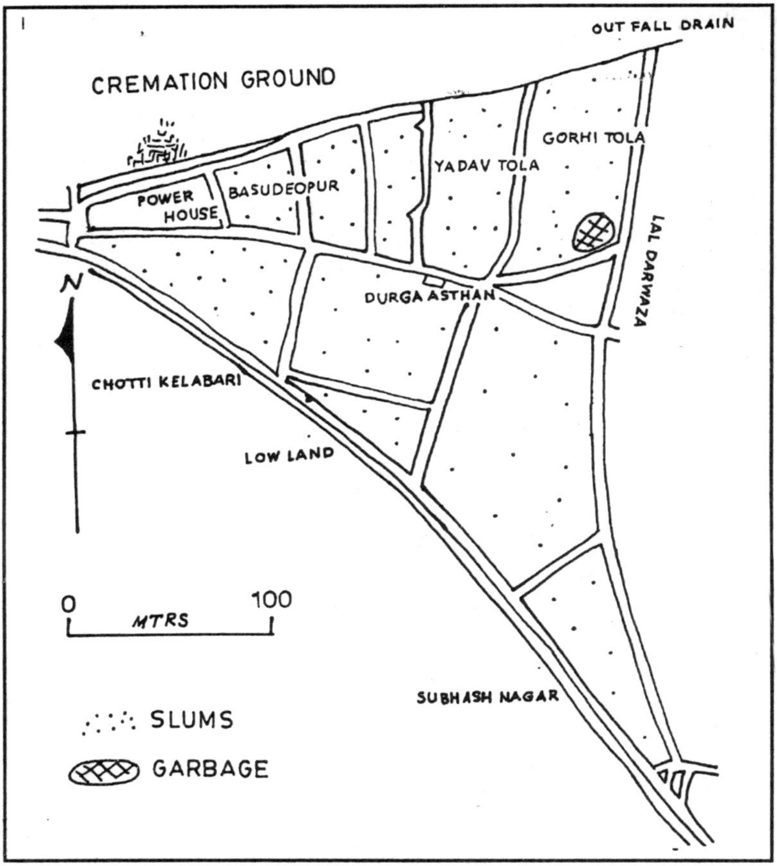

Fig. 8.2 : Slums Area of Laldarwaza Munger

Vegetable Cultivation

From Laldarwaja station upto Gumti No. 2, just on the northeast of the Railway line and water drain in the lowlying area, the field for vegetable cultivation lies. They are very productive for potato, brinjal, ladies finger, cabbage, beans, maize and several other vegetables.

Heaps of Garbage

In this *mohalla,* the dump of garbage has not been seen anywhere because people are careful enough with the help of ward commissioner to throw it outside *mohalla* just by the side of Puram Ganji Mill Road in the Ganga diara.

Residents of this Area

"Residents of this *mohalla* are of mixed quality." Some are rich, some are poor. And in the caste structure, Yadava, Kayastha, Gorhi and at some places Sahu and Brahmins are also living in Laldarwaja. In the central point of the *mohalla* Durgasthan is located and Laldarwaja station may be considered at the nodal point because it serves the people of entire city of Munger besides those who come from North Bihar to catch train from Jamalpur.

General Problems of the *Mohalla*

1. The refuge wastewater gets out from the main drain whose base is generally high from the local level. For this fact the flow of water is very slow and it dampens the area.
2. The cleaning and digging refuge water drain has not been done regularly.
3 In the following area water drains are required and their connection with the main drain is also essential for draining refuse water of the area preferably:
   (a) Sona Singh Lane (on the main road from Chhotelal Sharma's house upto Yugal Bihari Singa's house);
   (b) Inside Dhobi Tola;
   (c) From the Gate of Power House upto Fakira Yadava's house;
   (d) From Purana Ganji Mill upto Krishna Prasad Sinha and Suresh Yadava's house;
   (e) From old gymnasium upto Ram Bhaju Yadava's house.
   (f) From left Rameshwar Yadava's house upto Kishan Yadava's house.
4. They spray phenyl regularly as it is quite essential to keep the mosquitoes off on the settlement area.
5. Laldarwaja *mohalla* is quite free from heaps of garbage due to the conscious activities of the Ward Commissioner and local people.

6. The people of the area are of the opinion that more hand-cart is needed to clean the garbage. The tractor of municipal corporation rarely comes to collect the garbage.
7. Laldarwaja *mohalla* completely lacks service latrine due to conscious activities of ward commissioner and Municipality has no arrangement to clean the latrine and to set up new point of public latrine.
8. Uptil now M.P.s and M.L.As have not done any work for the development of Laldarwaja *mohalla.*
9. Laldarwaja has one Girl's Primary School. The lady teacher quite often engages herself in knitting sweater, shawl without caring about fate of the students.
10. In Laldarwaja *mohalla* the outbreak of Cholera, Kalazar and diarrhoea are common diseases.
11. The area is completely lacks of safe drinking and electricity.
12. Population of the area increases manifold and only the old five inches pipe is running in the area to supply drinking water in order to solve the problem. The diameter of the main pipe and frequency of drinking water supply should be increased.

The above information regarding problems of Laldarwaja Slum area has been given by Fuleshwar Yadav, Ward Commissioner.

ARGARA

Argara Slum Area

Argara slum area comes under ward No. 21 of Munger Municipality. It is bounded by Bari Bazar in the north, Bara in the south and the *mohalla* of Belda Bari in the West and Between Bazar in the front. The dominated castes of the area are Mehtar and other backward class people (Fig. 8.3).

Lanes

The *mohalla* is covered by various lanes and streets, which are rectangular and triangular in shape. In the northern part water works cover a big chunk of land followed by different *mohallas* like Gola Road, Bari Sangat Road, Between Bazar, Jamalpur Road etc.

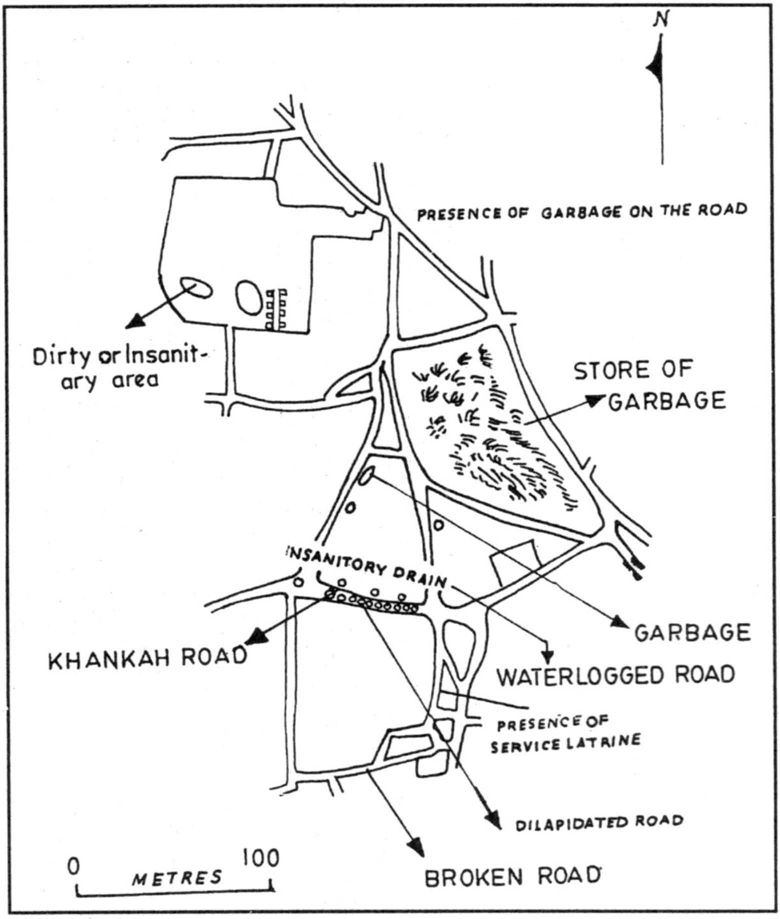

Fig. 8.3 : Slum Area of Argara Munger

Problems of Argara

In a *mohalla* like Argara the lack of metalled road and waterlogging are some of the common problems of the area. People of the area wanted to lessen the problem but the situations do not improve much. In the western part, the problem of waterlogging and water supply is a common problem of daily cleaning of roads and lanes. Although, the poor doe not get much but in some pockets the problems are so acute that it is going on from one part of the urban centre to the other. It may be problematic but with the help of the staff assistance the problem may be solved by collecting the garbage at a fixed place especially in a canasta. At some places the area also suffers from service latrine and at others the heaps of garbage and night soil on the roads, which are deteriorate the urban environment. The numbers of slum and squatter people are not too much but some of them arise due to cover congestion of houses and inadequate supply of water besides the area has been occupied by Mehtar people who are squatters.

Quality of Life in the Marketing Area of Khalifabag Chowk

Objective of Study

The notion of shopping behaviour is not a new concept but it is the outcome of the beginning of the urban culture. Due to the overwhelming growtlh of population and urbanization in the urban centre, the pattern of consumer behaviour is the matter of great concern for the sellers, buyers and economists on the other hand.

Consumer behaviour is studied so that shopping intensity could be ascertained along with the buyers behaviour accordingly. The type and pattern of the market should also be known for the planned development of the city.

The purpose of its study is to throw light on the trip behaviour pattern at Khalifabag Chowk in the city of Bhagalpur. George Ketona said that consumer psychology is the study of "The dynamics of the behaviour of mass of consumer."

The notion of shopping behaviour is analyzed in terms of location and number of shops and the consumer's travel and their location in the hinterland as they are the matter of concern for both sellers and buyers. The movement of consumer in and around the urban centre is guided by the purchasing power of the consumer, availability, quantity and price of goods, trip behaviour and the distance and time which a customer covers in making his trip. Generally, the customers of the nearby areas make multiple trip to the market and the item of purchase is very limited, on the other hand the customers of a distant place have selected multipurpose to the large Urban Centres.

Shopping behaviour is associated with the buying of products and services and the reason underlay in these activities. Shopping behaviour can be explained by identifying and studying all these factors, which influence the behaviours.

Customers usually purchase goods or makes their selection from goods displayed by a retailer.

Marketing decisions on activities are strongly influenced by the environmental factors. These external factors, i.e. competition, sociological, economics, political and the preference of an individual close friends and associates strongly affect the individuals, shopping behaviour.

Under the shopping behaviour the trip behaviour of the customer available from the urban to rural area for the purchase of goods is considered along with the distance travelled, area served, productivity of the region and the demand for the particular goods including accessibility. Generally, with greater accessibility the customers, trip is found to be maximum where as in an area of lesser accessibility they try to purchase a number of items from the market in a single trip.

Khalifabag Chowk

The Central business area of Khalifabag Chowk lies at a respectable distance from the Mahadeo Talkies and it is the main shopping centre of the city. This market i.e. Khalifabag Chowk extends upto Rajendra Prasad Road in the east, Variety Chowk in South, R.P. Road in the West and Kharman Chowk in the cross road where all sides are full of shops. It is one of the biggest markets of the city where a variety of goods are available in market in a small area. The present outline of the city gives a scope of planned development of road and shops on gridiron pattern. Such morphological conditions made the Chowk area more accessible from all the directions.

In this central business area the location of shops there is no separate compartment for each type of shop. Mixed pattern i.e. grocery, general stores, readymade garments, motels, pan, beverage shops, fruit stalls and others are found.

On Khalifabag Chowk both rural and urban customers come to purchase a variety of goods. The total number of shops are 950. This cause lots of inconvenience for double traffic. Figure 8.4 shows the intensity of central place hierarchy of the retail market in and around the Khalifabag Chowk, Bhagalpur.

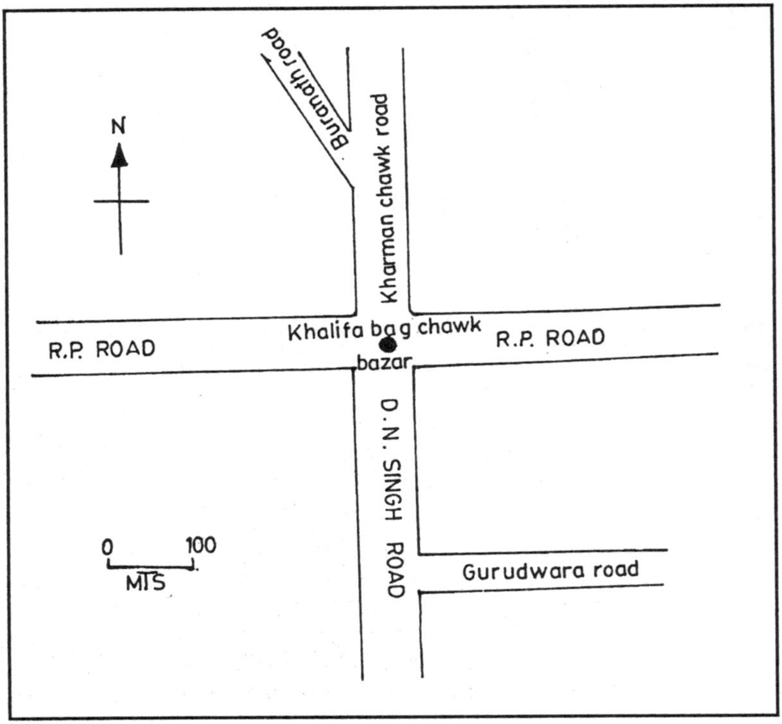

Fig. 8.4 : Khalifabag Chowk Bazar, Bhagalpur

Chitra Sala Studio is located on the northern eastern part of Khalifabag Chowk, Marwari Pathsala on the Eastern Part, Mahadeo Cinema in the West and Shiv Mandir in the south and Lajpat Park of the northern side of Khalifabag Chowk. Most of these markets are developed around Khalifabag Chowk Bazar area and have subsidiary link with the Khalifabag Chowk Bazar (Fig. 8.4).

Above figure highlights the location of residential and commercial buildings in the Khalifabag Chowk, Bhagalpur. Most of the areas are covered with houses and the only difference is that of functions carried on in these houses. The number of residential houses and its shortage could be seen in Table 8.2. The shortage of houses has been calculated on the basis of 3 persons per room, which should be a standard for a developing country like India. At present the occupancy rate is 7 persons per room.

Table 8.1: Khalifbagh Chowk: Types of Shops, Capital Involved (2005)

Sl. No.	*Types of Shop*	*Capital in Rupees*	*Daily Turn over*	*Profit Ratio*	*Nature of G/R*
1.	Central Stores	1,50,000	100-20000	6000	75/ 25
2.	Tea Stall	2,000	500	200	U
3.	Grocery Shop	75,000	1000	500	50/50
4.	Readymade Garments	5,00,000	15000	2000	70/30
5.	Radio and T.V.	4,00,000	15000	2000	75/25
6.	Books and Stationary	3,00,000	4000	2000	75/25
7.	Restaurants	5,00,000	5000	3000	60/40

Table 8.2 : Number of Residential Houses and its Shortage Khalifabag Chowk

Area	*No. of Houses*	*Population*	*Person per Room*	*Shortage of Houses*
Kotwali Chowk	500	5390	7	230
Variety Chowk	800	15000	6	50
Kharman Chowk	500	10050	5	250
Ghantaghar Chowk	400	8100	6	50
Total	2200	38540	24	550

Area, Population and Traffic Flow

The Khalifabag Chowk of Bhagalpur has an area of 92 hectares with a population 20240 in 2005. This comprises the residential and commercial sectors at Khalifabag Chowk, Variety Chowk, Kharman Chowk, Kotwali Chowk, and Ghantaghar Chowk besides the open shopping counters of Khalifabag Chowk (Fig. 8.5).

Figure 8.6 shows various sectors of Khalifabag Chowk, Bhagalpur. The area is surrounded by Kotwali Chowk in the western side, Ghantaghar Chowk in the eastern side, and Kharman Chowk on the northern side and Variety Chowk in the southern part of Khalifabag Chowk (Fig. 8.6).

With the help of Table 8.3 it is quite apparent that Khalifabag Chowk area contains 92 hectares of land with a population of 20240 (2005), which gives a population density of 517 per hectare. The study area has 950 shops unevenly distributed in various sectors in and around Khalifabagh Chowk, Bhagalpur.

Table 8.3 shows that the density of population in Khalifabagh Chowk, Bhagalpur. It has been found that the highest density 650 comes for Variety Chowk followed by 460 in Kotwali Chowk, 510 in Kharman Chack, 450 in Ghantaghar Chowk, etc.

Table 8.3 : Population, Area and Population Density of the Various Sectors of Khalifabag Chowk :2005

Sectors	*Area in Hectare*	*Population*	*Density per Hec.*	*No. of Shops*
Kotwali Chowk	33	5390	460	150
Variety Chowk	23	15000	650	600
Kharman Chowk	23	10050	510	150
Ghantaghar Chowk	13	8100	650	50
Total	92	38540	2070	950

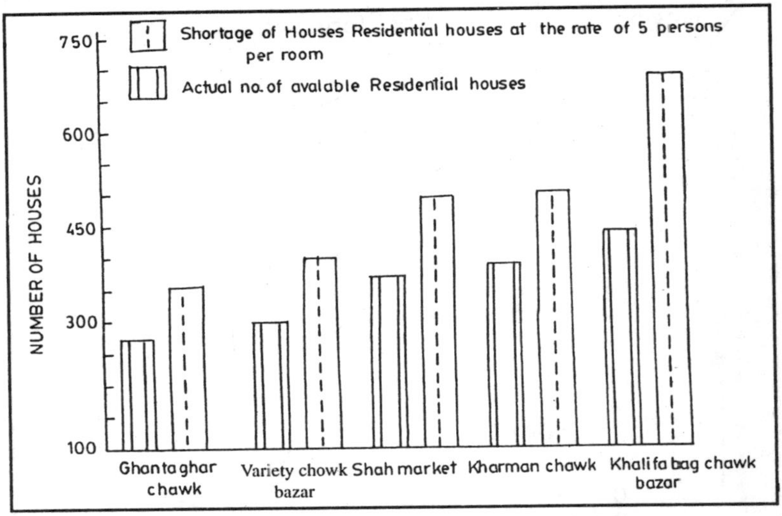

Fig. 8.5 : Khalifabag Chowk Bazar Bhagalpur, Shortage of Residential Houses

In these areas the density of population is very high because people are engaged in commercial activities in multistoried buildings and even in shopping areas the residential and commercial activities are going on in the same house. The ground floor (Fig. 8.7) is engaged in shopping activities and the floor is engaged in residential function.

Figure 8.8 and Table 8.4 shows that the traffic flow on the Khalifabag Chowk of Bhagalpur counted on the 15th September 2005 with the help of three classmates as helpers. 12 O'clock in the day back to the same time on the next day. Cyclist, Rickshaw, Paddlers, Scooters, Maruti which are the main traffic of the Khaifabag Chowk area (Table 8.4).

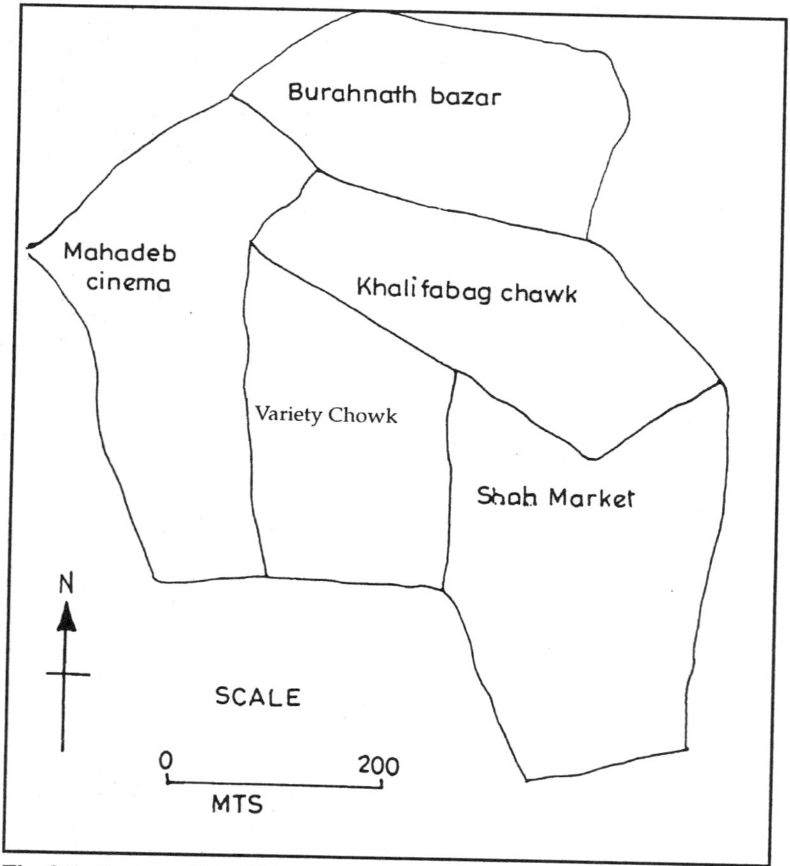

Fig. 8.6 : Sectors of Khalifabag Chowk Bazar

With the help of Table 8.4 it is quite apparent that Khalifabagh Chowk, Bhagalpur has about 15500 pedestrians per day, 5000 cyclist, 2000 rickshaw peddlers, 1400 scooter, 100 buses, about 400 cars and some times there are 2-3 bullock-carts pass through the Khalifabagh Chowk. It is quite clear that from 11 in the night upto 5 in the morning the number of the traffic is generally very low during the night hours. Two peak hours are 10 to 1 in the day and again 4 to 8 in the evening because during these hours the number of pedestrians and cyclist surpass all other traffic on Khalifabag Chowk.

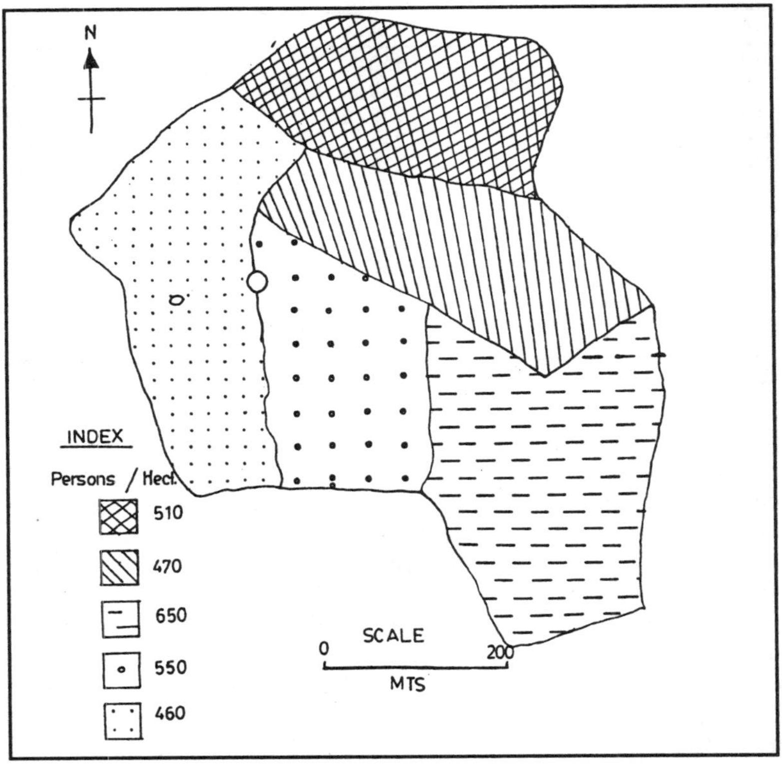

Fig. 8.7 : Khalifabag Chowk Bazar, Bhagalpur Population Density (2005)

Patterns of Consumer Behaviour

Cities do not grow by themselves. The countryside sets the task that must be performed in the City. The concept is first of all ensured by Mark Jefferson (1916). Christaller while studying the central place hierarchy found that the smaller cities have lesser number of consumer and the consumers behaviour is simple marked with single trip lesser purchasing capacity and short distance travel. The range of goods as suggested by Christaller is also much smaller in such markets. In comparison with this, in large centres the massive turnout of consumers with the multipurpose trips, long distance travel and bulk purchase are the points of difference at the same time, which is also helped by the range of goods. It has been suggested that all the goods of the

Table 8.4 : Number of Traffic on Khalifabagh Chowk

Hours	*Pedestrians*	*Cyclist*	*Rickshaw*	*Scooter*	*Bus*	*Cars*
06-07	503	300	150	75	20	10
10-11	1500	500	250	111	15	59
12-01	1620	475	235	105	10	39
02-03	1650	495	245	111	17	53
03-04	1735	509	275	131	20	57
04-05	2050	607	312	152	18	61
05-06	2152	619	317	163	9	62
06-07	2149	593	292	189	3	45
07-08	2013	528	287	202	1	39
10-11	2824	212	105	115	1	19
11-12	500	23	29	43	0	5
12-01	65	3	4	3	0	2
Total	15282	4864	2340	1400	114	441

lower order centres are found in the large central places and hence the complexity of functions, morphological structure and wide zone of consumer are the rule of Christalle's hierarchy of central places for both the inter city central places and the intracity central places.

On the other hand, it favoured the idea of Christaller but suggested that all the goods of lower order centre should not necessarily be found in the higher order centre. On the basis of consumer movement and the delimitation of upland of a city the hierarchy of the central place can easily be achieved.

Trip Behaviour

Figure 8.9 shows the trip behaviour of the Khalifabagh Chowk Bazar in the city of Bhagalpur 2003. It has been found that on all the dispersed location or neighbourhood store only the local people visit to the shop whereas on business trips on mostly station or different residential areas of the city purchase some of the specialised goods located in the special market and local shopping centres like Shah market, Lohapatti market, Marwari tola market, Ganapatti Plaza market, Station Chowk market, Lahari tola market and other.

It has been found that consumers generally come to the Shah market from a far off places besides the non-basic population of the city of Bhagalpur. The total daily arrival of consumer is only 83 in case of the electronic instruments and 387 in case of grocery shops.

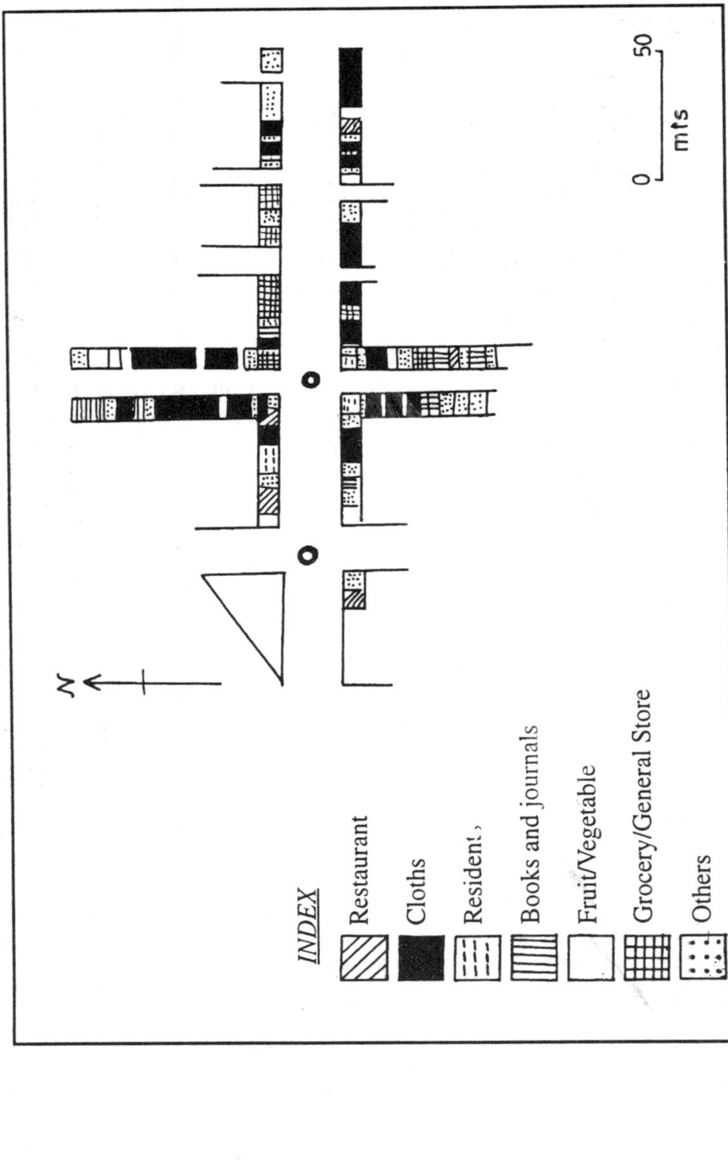

Fig. 8.8 : Busines Structure of Khalifabag Chowk, Bhagalpur

This shows that Bhagalpur is a developing market having backward people with low purchasing power. This also shows that useless the population of the region compels the quality of shopping centre will not increase in the near future. So far as the prospect of the planning is concerned it also warrants the planner to involve large amount of capital for city planning with special reference to better shopping centres (Fig. 8.9).

Analysis of Consumer Behaviour in the Upland of Bhagalpur

The study of consumer behaviour pattern has been contemplated through fieldwork in the upland of Bhagalpur in 2005. In this investigation it has been found that the supply of vegetables, milk, dried cowdung and other essential items produced in the vicinity of the urban areas are generally meant for sale for the city residents.

The zone of supply of cloth, medicines and other items of higher order goods in the city of Bhagalpur is larger in comparison with the above. This is due to the attractive market, cheap goods; chance of the availability of higher order goods in one trip makes the zone of influence larger in comparison with the above.

Age Group and Shopping Behaviour

By categorising the types of shops we can find out the special pattern of consumer behaviour, age group of consumers and their respective behaviour given in Table 8.5.

(i) Hotel, restaurants and entertainment or dance.
(ii) Food, clothing and grocery.
(iii) Medicine and cultural purposes.

Table 8.5 : Age Structure of People Visiting the Shop (2005)

Age Group	*Categories of Shop Visited in*			
	Type (i)	*Type (ii)*	*Type (iii)*	*Total*
14-23 years	50	20	20	90
24-50 years	30	50	30	110
50 and above years	20	30	50	100

Retail Business Structure and Shopping Plan

There is a perplexing variety of retail trading houses judged from the point of view of these places of business they may be categorised as:

(i) Itinerant or mobile retail traders, and
(ii) Fixed shop retailers.

These two broad categories and their divisions may be shown as following. (Fig 8.9 and 8.10)

Retailers

ITINERANT	SMALL SCALE	LARGE SCALE
(1) Hawkers and Pedlars	(1) Street Stall Holder	(1) Departmental Stores
(2) Cheap Jack	(2) Second-hand Goods	(2) Multiple Shops
(3) Market Graders	(3) General Shops	(3) Co-operative Stores
	(4) Speciality Shops	(4) Mail Order House
		(5) Hire-purchases Shops

Fig. 8.9 : Khalifabag Chowk Mobile Retail Traders

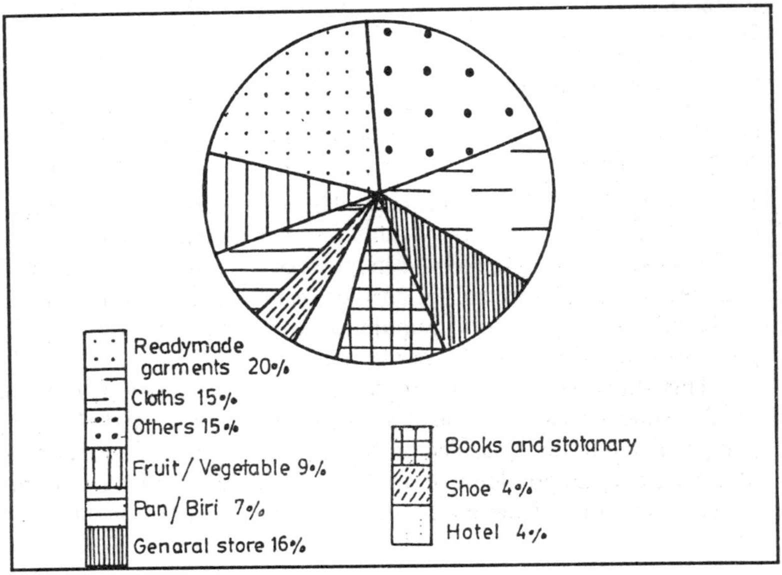

Fig. 8.10 : Khalifabag Chowk Retail Business Structure

Table 8.6 : Khalifabag Chowk: Types and Number of Shops

Nature of Shops	*No. of Shops*
1. Readymade Garments	40
2. Cloth Shops	32
3. Fruit Stalls	19
4. Vegetables Shops	10
5. Boot Houses	12
6. Hotels and Restaurant	7
7. Books	6
8. Journals and Magazines	5
9. Stationary	6
10. Watches	5
11. Pan, Biri, Cigarette	13
12. Oil Mills	1
13. Earthen Jars	2
14. Calendar Stall	4
15. Decorating Shops	1
16. Utensil Shops	5
17. Tailoring Shops	4
18. Gun Shops	3
19. Tea Stalls	4
20. Electrical Goods	4
21. Spectacle Shops	4
22. Lottery	1
23. Bag Shops	3
24. Glass Store	3
25. Mosquito Net Shops	3
26. T.V. and Radio Shops	5
Total	204

Source : Field Work.

Khalifabag Chowk Bazar is the central business area of the Bhagalpur city. The shopping behaviour of this area has aroused a keen interest to study the shopping behaviour in terms of attracting the consumers and the quantity of turnover of business establishment. It has an area of 92 hectares and a total population of 38,540 and the average population density is 20,070 per hectare.

This study has been contemplated in close associations with the retail business structure, consumer behaviour pattern and shopping plan available in the area. The problems of the area such as, shortage of houses and the problems of drinking water and the electric supply. Hence, each area of the market has a different pattern of quality of life.

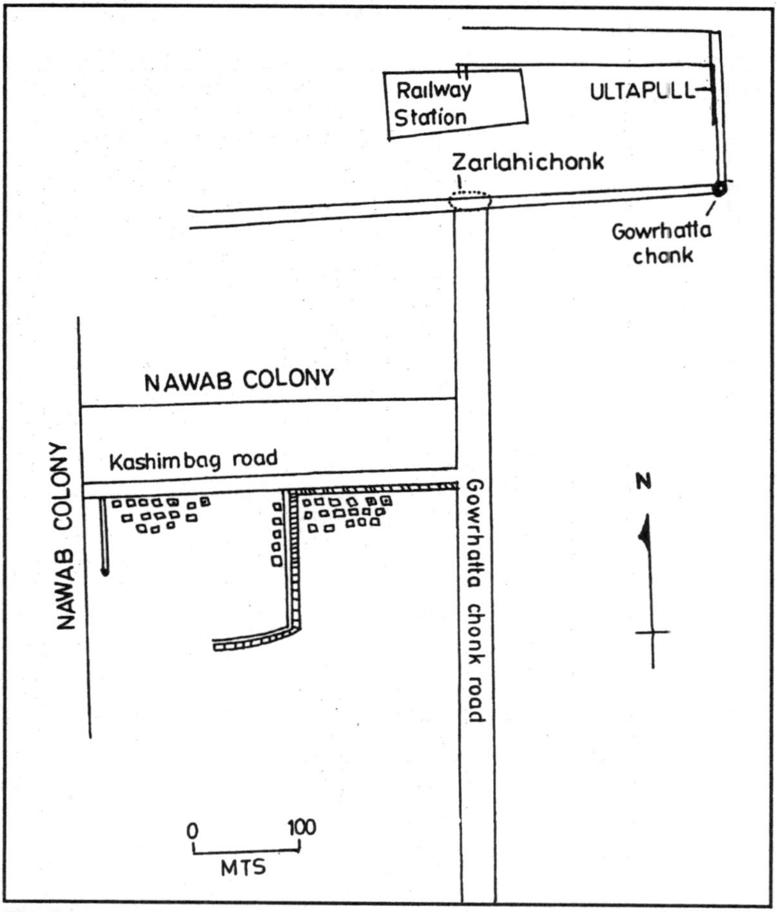

Fig. 8.11 : Location and Boundary of Kasimbag

Quality of Life in Kasimbag Slum Area of Bhagalpur

Slums are the main problems of Bhagalpur city, which pose obstacle in urban management. These problems can be solved only by well planned urban development. Hence, the assessment and analysis of slums are essential for the economic study. Thus socio-economic study of slum becomes most important in the present scenario of urbanization.

The present study is a modest attempt to assess and analyse the slum and squatters of Bhagalpur city.

Kasimbag in ward No. 13 is located in the central part of Bhagalpur city on the southern bank of the Ganga river. About two decades ago it was an open land and neglected place. Low income group people come here to settle. They began to earn their livelihood by pulling rickshaws and washing clothes. They purchased the land at low prices. The relatives of the inhabitants also come here to settle and co-operated in the enhancement of slum with low standard of living (Fig. 8.11) untouchables and they have lived in insanitary environment where pigs have further deteriorated the environment.

The biggest problems are poverty and unemployment, which create an environment of slums and squatter settlement. These people have got very meagre amount for the upgrading of slums. The government has constructed about 60 houses for the slum people, but they are so small that a family of 8 to 10 persons cannot get proper adjustment in one room. It may be hoped that the situation will improve in future.

REFERENCES

Aranganannal: Socio-economic Survey of Madras Slums (1971. Survey), Madras: Tamilnadu Slum Clearnce Board, 1975.

Bharat Sevak Samaj: Slums of Old Delhi: Atma Ram and Sons, 1958.

Desai, A.R. and Pillai, S.D. (1972), *A Profile of An Indian Slum,* Bombay: University of Bombay.

Dubey, Binod (1990), "They Grow Up and Die in Streets Patna Slum III, *Times of India,* 25th August 1990.

Lynch, Owen M. (1974), "Political Mobilization and Ethnicity Among Adi-Dravidas in Bombay Slum" in *Economic and Political Weekly*, IX (39): 1974 September 28.

Nambiar, P.K. (1906), Slum in Madras City, *Census of India*, 1961, Vol. IX, and Madras Part XI-C, 1906.

Singh U. (1966), "Geographical Analysis of Slum Areas in Indian Cities with Special Reference to Kanpur," *National Geographical Journal of India*, 1966, 12, 178-187.

Stokes, Charles, J. (1962), "A Theory of Slums," *Land Economics,* Vol. 38 (3), August, pp. 187-197, *Sunday Standard* (1973): Madras.

Subrahmanyam, N. (1940), 'Problems of Sub-Urban Municipality with Special Reference to Saidapet,' *Journal of Madras Geographical Association*, 1940, 15, 19-29.

Unni, K. Raman (1977), "Slum Relocation and Urban Planning" in *Social Action*, Vol. 27. No. 4. October-December.

Venkatarayappa, K. (1972), *Slums, Delhi*; Sterling.

Wiebe, Paul D. (1975), *Social Life in An Indian Slum,* Delhi: Vikas Publishing House.

9 MATERNAL AND CHILD HEALTH IN SLUM AREA : A Case Study

In recent years there has been a growing concern for women's health in developing countries. This is evident from the adoption of women's health opersepectives in strategies addressing child survival, family planning and women's development issues. This concern has created a demand for information that can provide a diagnosis of women's health needs in developing countries. The intermediate variables which affect women's health include the woman's health bearing pattern, he use of health services, and her health related practices that affect her susceptibility. A woman's child bearing pattern related to her age at child bearing episodes, the number of pregnancies and births, and the extent of birth spacing, studies have shown that the prevalence of reproductive morbidity is higher in the early and late child bearing years, and increases the number of pregnancies and births and with shorter birth intervals.

The extent of a woman's use of health services during pregnancies, at the time of delivery and during the postpartum period, are important factors in preventing most of the complications and health problems associated with child bearing. A woman's health related behaviour, particularly during pregnancy, affects the like likelihood of her suffering from reproductive morbidity. Poverty an economic hardship compel many people to migrate to urban areas resulting in large number of slums and squatter settlements in these areas. The overwhelming majority of slum dwellers lack proper housing, piped water and facilities for the removal of household and human waste. Family planning and mother and child health care services can improve the survival and quality of life of mothers and children but are often under utilised by those who are in greatest need. This is particularly true of slum areas where child mortality is high because the burden of disease is greater and services are less easily available.

The utilisation of health services is a complex behavioural phenomenon related to the organization of the health delivery system, and is affected by the availability, quality, costs, continuity and comprehensiveness of services. Social structure and health beliefs also affect the use of health services. For preventive services like prenatal care, family planning or immunisation, the perception of need is more complicated than in the case of disease, and involves beliefs about the susceptibility to, and the consequences and effectiveness of the intervention.

The outbreak of diseases such as dysentery, diarrhoea, typhoid etc. is common. Children are particularly susceptible to diarrhea and dysentery which result in high infant and child mortality. Malnutrition among the slum population, and in particular among children, and pregnant and lactating women is also severe. According to a study conducted by the centre for urban studies, about 30 to 40 per cent of urban slum dwellers suffer from disease at any given point of time. Children and mothers are more vulnerable than other to diarrhoea, respiratory tract infections, scabies, fever, typhoid, whooping cough and various eye diseases. And, health services are inadequate to meet their needs.

The purpose of the present chapter is to study the health of mother and children living in the slums of Bhagalpur and Munger towns and to identify the factors which influence their health as also groups who are at risk because of inadequate services, with a view to instituting measures for improvement.

Data Source

According to a survey conducted by the 50 urban health volunteers' programme, there were about 2,156 slums in Bhagalpur and Munger towns. The total estimated number of slum households was 1,26,392 with an estimated population of 7,18,000. Using this information, a two-stage cluster sampling technique is used to obtain required sample.

At the first stage, four blocks were selected randomly from a list of 24 blocks. In the second stage, five per cent of the slums in these four blocks were selected randomly. Thus, 30 slum area were selected randomly from the sampling frame. A total of 1,291 women in the reproductive age were interviewed from 1,323 selected slum households. The information on both socio-economic and environmental characteristics of the women was collected.

Socio-Economic Profile

Table 9.1 presents the socio-economic and environmental characteristics of the women.

On an average, the women were slightly over 29 years of age and had 1.3 years of schooling. As many as 73 per cent were illiterate. Their husbands had a comparatively better educational level with and average of about three years of education. About a quarter of the husbands were in service, followed by rickshaw/cart puller (16.0 per cent, salesman (8.1 per cent), and petty businessman (7.5 per cent). None of the slum households had their own latrine facility and 9 per cent used drains as latrines.

The disposal of solid waste also posed a major problem. As seen from Table 9.1, ever two-fifths of the respondents (42 per cent) used a fixed place provided by the Municipal Corporation for disposal of solid waste, 21 per cent used an open place for disposing solid waste, while the 19 per cent had no fixed place for the purpose. Access to cooking fuel was another major problem, most of the slum dwellers had little access to cooking gas only ten per cent.

Table 9.1 : Socio-economic Profile of Women

(Percentage)

Education	*Women*	*Husbands*
Mean age : 29.2 years		
None	72.5	57.9
1-5 years	20.5	18.5
6-9 years	6.3	13.9
10-12 years	0.7	8.2
13+years	—	1.5
Mean years of schooling	1.3	2.8
Husband's occupation		
Service		25.9
Rickshaw/cart puller		16.0
Salesman		8.2
Petty business		7.5
Other		48.5
Unemployed		2.9
Average monthly household income : Take 2.545		
House		46.0
Bamboo and CI sheet		2.8
Semi-*pucca*		29.8

(Contd.)

Table 9.2 *(Contd.)*

Thatched	12.9
Other	11.3
Sources of Drinking water	
Municipal pipe	76.4
Tube well	12.2
Neighbour	1.6
Other	9.8
Type of latrine	
Pucca	47.4
Kutcha	37.3
Drain	9.0
Open field	1.3
Other	5.1
Disposal of solid waste	
Fixed place of municipal corporation	42.2
Common place	13.0
Open place	20.6
No fixed place	4.8
Source of cooking fuel	
Kerosen/Wood	81.6
Pipe gas	10.3
Cylinder gas and electricity	1.6
Other	6.6
Lighting facility	
Kupi/Hurricane lamp	36.0
Rented connection	31.3
Regular connection	30.0
Other	2.7

Households had piped gas, while the vast majority (about 82 per cent) used kerosene/wood as cooking fuel. Similarly, access to electricity was limited to about 30 per cent of the households, a third of the households used traditional kupi/hurricane lamps.

Maternal and Child Health

Table 9.2 presents the fertility status, current pregnancy status and information about the last pregnancy and childbirth of the women and the immunisation status of the children.

Lifetime fertility was estimated through a sequence of questions. On average, each woman had given birth to 5.5 children of whom about two had been born in the slum. The average number of living children per woman was 4.4 of whom about 1.1 had died after the woman had moved to the slum.

Table 9.2 : Current Pregnancy Status : Reproductive Behaviour and Health Care Practices of Women

Average number of children ever born per woman			5.5
Average number of children ever born in the slum per woman			2.0
Average number of children per woman			4.4
Average number of children who had died in the slum			1.1
	Yes	10.1%	
	No	89.9%	
Mean duration of pregnancy at the time of survey (in month) 5.6			
Whether antenatal visit made			
	Yes	40.0	
	No	60.0	
Whether faced any problems during last pregnancy			
	Yes	8.4	
	No	91.6	
Type of problems faced during last delivery			
	Excessive pain		39.5
	Unconsciousness		29.0
	Bleeding		14.5
	Placenta problem		9.2
	Tetanus		1.3
	Cesarean		6.6
Whether visited doctor			
	Yes		32.1
	No		67.9
Type of person who assisted last childbirth			
	Untrained *dai*		52.0
	Relatives		20.3
	Doctor/ Nurse		11.1
	Trained *dai*		2.4
	Neighbour		1.3
	None		
Place of delivery of last child			
	Own house		79.7
	Hospital		10.3
	Relative's		10.0
Whether ever breastfed youngest child			
	Yes		98.0
	No		2.0
Mean duration of breast feeding (months) 24.0			
Whether colostrums given to the youngest child			
	Yes		46.5
	No		53.5
Current use status of FP			
	Yes		38.5
	No		64.5

A little over 10 per cent of the women were pregnant at the time of survey, the mean duration of pregnancy being 5.6 months. Among the pregnant women, only about 39 per cent for an antenatal checkup, and about the same percentage had been immunised. The findings also indicated that about 8 per cent of the women with children under five years of age had experienced problems during their last pregnancy, and only one-third of the main problems were excessive pain (39.5 per cent), spells of unconsciousness (29.0 per cent), and excessive bleeding (14.5 per cent). The majority of the births (about 80 per cent) had occurred at home, and more than half (52 per cent had been attended by untrained *dais* and one-fifth (23 per cent) by relatives/ neighbours. Only about 15 per cent had received trained birth assistance.

That breastfeeding is universal in Bihar was also corroborated by our feedings. 98 per cent of the women had breastfed their youngest child, and the average duration of breastfeeding was 24 months.

Less than half of the youngest children had been given colostrums. The findings also indicated that almost three-fifths (58 per cent) of all children under five years of age had been immunized. Further, about 39 per cent of the women were using a contraceptive at the time of the interview.

Maternal and Child Morbidity and Mortality

Table 9.3 summarises the findings relating to the morbidity and mortality among the slum women and their children. About 40 per cent of the women reported that they were suffering from some form of ailment at the time of interview. Table 9.3 indicates the most common was non-specific pain (28 per cent). Again, only 75 per cent of those who reported these ailments, by and large from medical practitioners (62 per cent).

As regards their children's health, about 32 per cent of the women reported that their children were suffering from various ailments at the time of survey (Table 9.3). The most common ailments were fever/ cold (18.5 per cent), diarrhoea (16.3 per cent), skin diseases (14.3 per cent) and cough (9.3 per cent). A vast majority of the children about four-fifths had been treated for their ailments.

Table 9.3 : Morbidity and Mortality Among Women and Children

Whether mothers suffered from any disease	
Yes	39.7
No	60.3
Type of sickness	
Pain	28.5
Fever	16.6
Gastric ulcer	8.0
Fever/Cold	6.5
Skin disease	6.5
Malnutrition	5.1
Cough	4.5
Diarrhoea	4.3
Heart disease	3.1
Jaundice	2.9
Respiratory problems	2.2
Tuberculosis	1.6
Others	10.2
Whether treatment received	
Yes	75.0
No	25.0
Place of seeking treatment	
Doctor/hospital	61.5
Kabiraj	4.4
Others	34.1
Whether children suffered from any disease at the time of survey	
Yes	32.0
No	68.0
Type of disease they suffer	
Fever	18.5
Diarrhoea	16.3
Fever/Cold	15.3
Skin disease	14.3
Cough	9.3
Worms	5.0
Chest pain	3.5
Breathing problems	3.0
Measles	1.9
Jaundice	1.9
Tuberculosis	1.9
Others	8.0
Whether treatment received	
Yes	78.9
No	21.1
Deaths of the children	
Under five	64.5
Above five	5.5

(Contd.)

Table 9.3 *(Contd.)*

Age of death	
Below 6 months	51.7
6-12 months	15.8
13-36 months	20.4
37-60 months	6.6
61 months and above	5.5
Mean age at death (years) : Place of death	
Slum	54.4
Village	45.5
Cause of death	
Diarrhoea	13.7
Tetanus Fever	12.3
Pneumonia	6.6
Measles	5.5
Fever/Cold	5.3
Small Pox	2.3
Malnutrition	2.0
Skin disease	1.8
Jaundice	1.3
Cough	1.0
Other	45.9

Almost all the women (95 per cent) had experienced child loss. More than half of the child deaths had occurred to children under six months and another 16 per cent to children between six and 12 months. Further, over half (54 per cent) of the child deaths had occurred after the women had come to reside in the slum.

An attempt to identify the cause of child deaths pointed to diarrhoea and tetanus as the major causes; one in seven children and one in eight children had died due to diarrhoea and tetanus respectively. Other reported causes of death included pneumonia, measles and fever.

Multivariate Analsis

Logistic regression analysis was used to identify the factors that related to the health of the women and their children. Currently married women having children aged less than five years were considered for the analysis. The results are presented in Table 9.4.

Table 9.4 : Logistic Regression Analysis

Variables		*Coefficient*	*Odds ratio*
X_1	Current use status	1.3645	1.440
	Own house/neighbour/relatives	—	—
X_2	Hospital, clinic/trained *dais*	0.0272	1.027
X_3	Income of the household (Taka)		
	< 3000	—	—
	> 3000	0.45 7	0.637
X_4	Whether health workers visited her	0.1007	0.904
X_5	Total children born alive		
	< 3	—	—
	> 3	0.0712	1.074
X_6	Age of the woman		
	<30	—	—
	>30	—	—
X_7	Whether ever attended school	0.2044	1.227
X_8	Whether received vaccination during pregnancy	0.7081	2.030
X_9	Type of birth assistance during last delivery		
	Untrained *dais*	—	—
	Nurse/trained *dais*	0.9627	2.169
X_{10}	Age of youngest child		
	18 months	—	—
	18-35	-.1473	0.863
	35-54	-.3339	0.716
	Constant	-2.7958	—
-2 log likelihood chi-square 404.50		*p*<.000	

Significant at 5 per cent level

Variables were assumed to influence internal and child health.

X_1 **Current contraceptive use status**

0 : If the woman is currently using a method

1 : If the woman is not currently using a method

X_2 **Place of delivery of last child**

0 : If last birth occurred at own house or at neighbour/relative's

1 : If last birth occurred at hospital/clinic/trained *dai*/nurse.

X_3 **Income of the household**

0 : If less than TK. 3000

1 : If more than TK. 3000

X_4 **Whether any health worker visited the respondent**
0: If a worker visited them
1 : If a worker did not visit them

X_5 **Total number of children born alive**
0 : for < 3 children
1 : for >3 children

X_6 **Age of the respondent**
0 : If it was < 30 years
1: If it was above 30 years

X_7 **Whether respondent ever attended school**
0 : If the woman ever attended school
1 : If the woman never attended school

X_8 **Whether respondent received vaccination during last pregnancy**
0 : If the woman receive vaccination
1 : If the woman did not receive vaccination

X_9 **Type of birth assistance during last pregnancy**
0 : If attend by untrained dai/relative/neighbour
1 : If attended by a trained dai/nurse

X_{10} **Age of the youngest child**
0 : If less than 18 months old
1 : If between 18-35 months old
2 : If a child is between 39-59 months

X_{11} **Whether the child is immunised**
0 : If not immunised
2 : If immunised

Among the variables considered, only two, namely vaccination of the pregnant woman and delivery by an untrained *dais* were found to be associated with maternal health problems. Mothers who do not receive vaccination complications related to pregnancy. In terms of problems experienced during pregnancy, and the vaccination status. Similarly, women who were attended by untrained *dais* during delivery were more likely to encounter pregnancy related problems. Although household income was not significantly associated with pregnancy related problems, the sign of the coefficient suggests that it has a negative effect. The higher income is the access to medical and other modern services, and the lower is the likelihood of health problems during pregnancy.

Discussion and Conclusion

The maternal and child health problems that exist in the slums are enormous. We know that having many children, at short intervals or at unfavourable maternal ages endangers the lives of both mother and child. In this situation, that a majority of the mother did not receive antenatal care, specifically during pregnancy resulted in various health problems during pregnancy. The utilization of untrained birth assistance, a common feature in the slums, was also associated with the reproductive health problems. A woman's postpartum amenorrhoea and her menstruating interval both tend to be shorter following the death of a child.

Hence, when a child dies seen after birth, the subsequent birth interval is generally shorter for both biomedical and behavioural reasons.

Logistic regression analysis suggests that lack of access to immunization of pregnant women and delivery of babies by untrained *dais* were the important factors contributing to the poor maternal and child health status in the slums.

There are also other reasons why urban slum women do not use public health care facilities. The women's informal responses to this question revealed that the health centres often run short of medical supplies, the waiting time at the public health facility is too lengthy, and that the medical personal are often unapproachable medical services and supplies. All these constraints should be taken into consideration for improving the health of workers and children form these deprived group.

REFERENCES

Dixon-Mueller, R. and Waserheit, J. (1991), The Culture of Silence : Reproductive Tract Infections Among Woman in the Third World. *International Women's Health Coalition*, New York.

Frodler. J. L. (1981), "A Review of the Literature on Access and Utilization of Medical Care with Special Emphasis Rural Primary Cares". *Social Science and Medicine* 50 :129-142.

Huda, Z. Hind, K., Nabil, Y. El. Monselhy, M. and Mohamed Fadle (1993), "Concepts and Measure of Reproductive Morbidity. Health Transition Review. *The Cultural Social and Behavioural Determinants of Health*. Vol.3, No. 1.

Kroger, A. (1983), "Anthropological and Socio-medical Health Care Research in Developing Countries" *Social Science and Medicine* 17 (3) : 147-161.

Resenstock, E. (1966), "Child Mortality and Fertility in Columbia: Individual and Community Effects", *Health Policy and Education*, Vol.2, 385.

UNICEF (1989) State of the World's Children, Oxford University Press, New York.

10 PROBLEMS AND PLANNING OF QUALITY OF LIFE

In this chapter discussions have been made regarding problems and prospects of urban life in the urban centres of Munger and Bhagalpur. The problems include poverty, misery, slum development, rise of squatter settlements, road holds up by the thieves. burglary, theft, flood, drought and vice of the underworlds are general issues affecting the urban life in the cities of Munger and Bhagalpur.

Among the prospects hope for the better life, planned development of colonies relocation and remodelling of slums, respite from the various kinks of diseases, supply of safe drinking water and the control of excessive population growth through preventive methods of family planning are important. The robbery on roads, killing spree by warning groups, snatching of motorcycles and kidnapping of boys and girls are important.

Now-a-days the urban societies of Munger and Bhagalpur have been divided into income group, caste, religions and several other sectors. The environmental situation is worse. The cultural variations and differences in the level of modernity are vast. The social cohesion lacks in the major urban centres like Munger and Bhagalpur. With the increase in population size of urban centre these gaps are so large that their vastness is increasing day by day. Hence, any conscious planning has to consider all these aspects so that our society of the cities of Munger and Bhagalpur could prosper in a right direction, without any ifs and buts. Unfortunately our efforts of planning have not been progressing properly due to lack of fund and dearth of enthusiasm.

Model Formulation

The problem of the cities of Munger and Bhagalpur has been related with growth of slum, improper development of transportation node, shortage of houses, problem of unemployment besides alcoholism, need of children's welfare, excessive a population growth and rise in the environmental pollution, etc. On the other hand planning will be to rehabilitate slum dwellers improve transport frequency, construction of new residential colonies and houses along with creation of new job opportunities. All these need strong determination to check alcoholism, creation of health centres, adoption of family planning measures and afforestation under social forestry programme (Fig. 10.1)

Recently, the cause of urban environment and its attributes of pollution affect the human being on a multi-pronged basis because increased interactions of human beings with the nature has created regional as well as ecological imbalances, the destruction of forests, dump of garbage, air, water and sound pollutions, abject poverty, refinement of crime and decrease of morale of people and the reclamation of wetlands are the major problems of urban social environment (Fig. 10.2).

The issues of urban development are related with lack of infrastructure facilities, stagnation of refuge water, political differences and turmoil, caste hatredness, income differentiation, illiteracy and superstitious belief among people besides dilapidated roads, rise of slum at places and squatter settlements to consider a few parameters (Fig. 10.3).

The problems of urban life are also associated with urban resource management, lack of proper and quick means of transport, lack of capital for business pursuits and industrial development, besides grabing of land, residential houses, shops and hard competition even for small pieces of land.

The planning for urban development and toning up the environment is a decision-making process for bridging the rural-urban gap of pollutants, enhancement of urban oriented resources, building of infrastructure facilities in the urban centres of Munger and Bhagalpur and ameliorating the environment by checking pollution for the betterment of the society. In the cities of Munger and Bhagalpur it has been observed that money, men and material flow from lower order strata of the society to urban core of the higher order. In these cities the incessant migration of rural folk have assumed such alarming proportions that they require immediate attention of the urban planners and other concerned authorities. Hoselitz (1959 p.231) has therefore, asked for an early application of rehabilitation and development plans

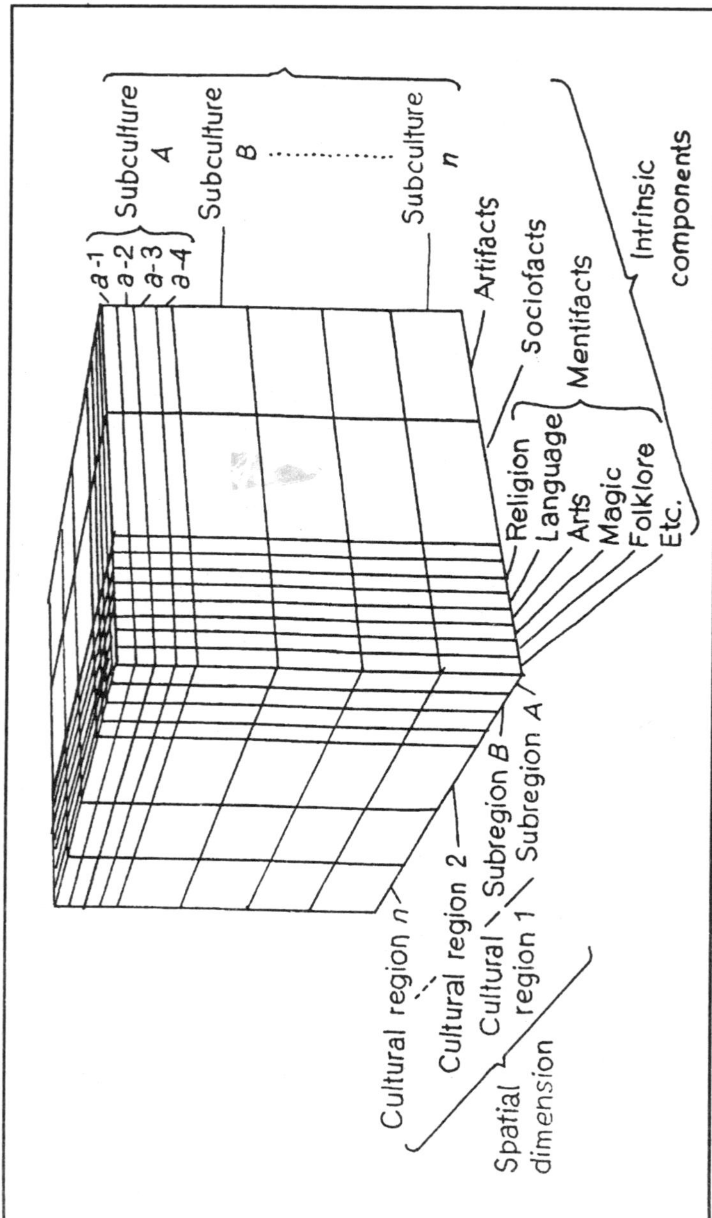

Fig. 10.1 : Huxley's Model of Culture and Quality of Life

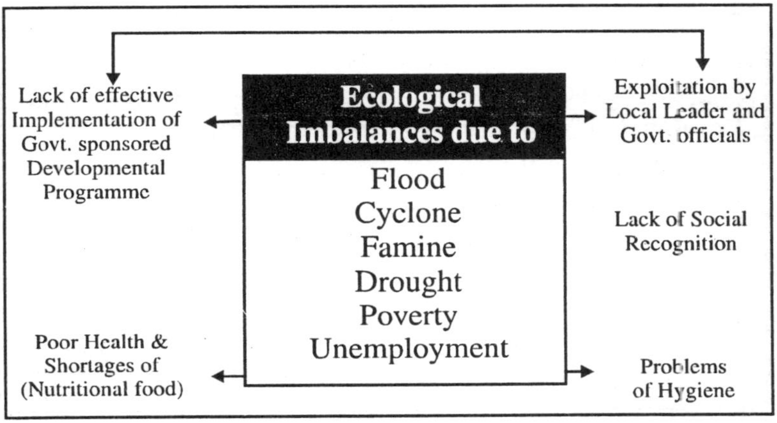

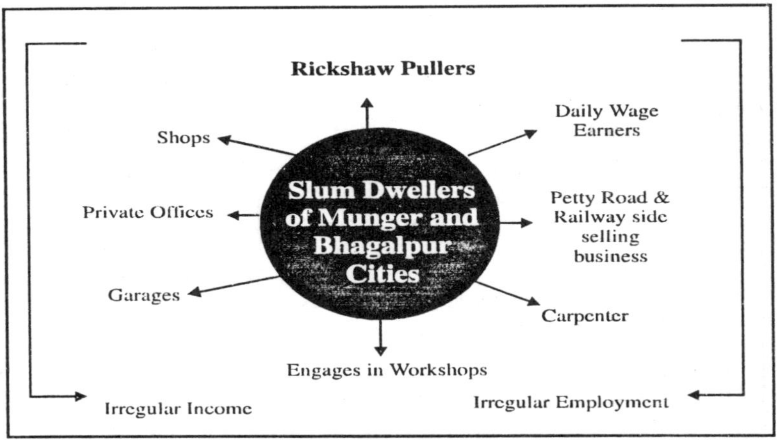

Fig. 10.2 : Slum Dwellers of Munger and Bhagalpur Cities

to Indian cities like Munger and Bhagalpur particularly in view of their heterogeneous character.

It is an established fact that the cities have more problems, which are typical in nature. Preparation of a town development plan requires consideration of former growth trends, existing conditions and probable future requirements. In this context, Wilson (1974, p.12) has noted three basic ingredients of planning, namely policy, design and analysis.

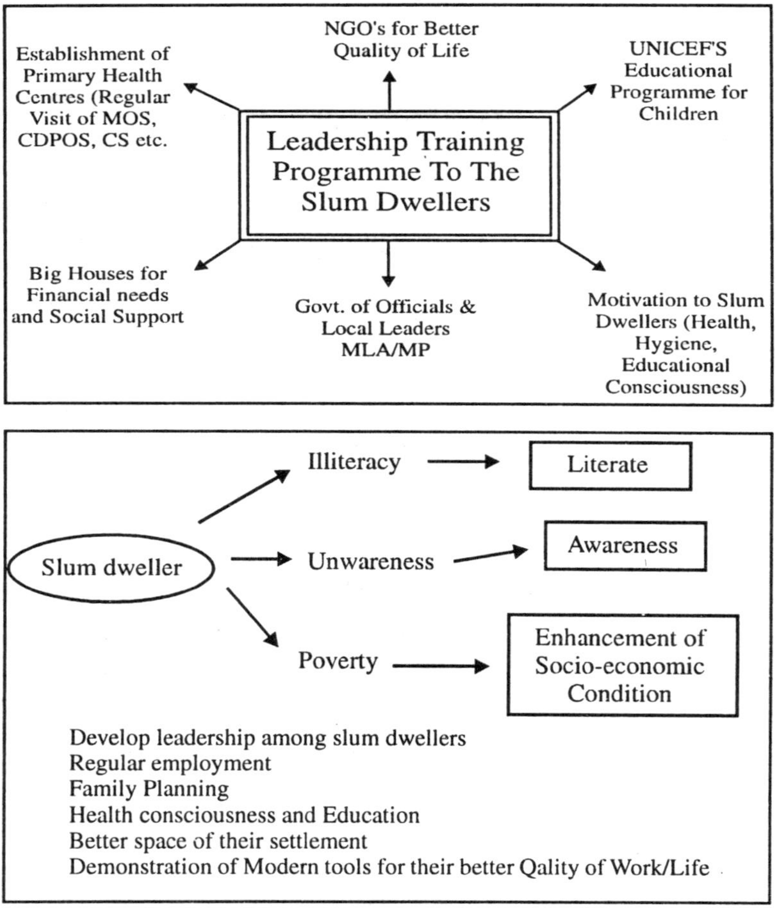

Fig. 10.3 : Ladership Training Programme to the Slum Dwellers

In this report, a conceptual framework has been proposed for a systematic study of the problems of Munger and Bhagalpur so that a comprehensive town development plan could be prepared. Emphases have been laid here not only on further expansion but also on the renovation of existing areas under residential, commercial and industrial uses, besides improvements in transportation facilities, street network, adoption of flood preventive measures and a variety of other public works. After an elaborate analysis of the problems associated with various land uses, a design has been provided for formulating town reconstruction and suggestions have been made in this regard. These steps are intimately and supplemented to each other. The capital required for the reconstruction of Munger and Bhagalpur needed proper legislation of the municipality and the government. Thus a comprehensive plan for the development of Munger and Bhagalpur has been proposed at grass root level.

Problems

The cities of Munger and Bhagalpur have experienced a tremendous growth of population during the last three decades (1971-2001). This gain in population is attributable to natural increase, migration from rural areas, and to some extent, the influx of refugees from the neighbouring Bangladesh. The excessive population migration from rural to urban areas has been an important phenomenon throughout the historic times. These phenomenal migrations are due to attractions of high standard of living and better social life. The rural settlements in close proximity of these cities have witnessed the recent impact of urbanization and soon these will be engulfed in the overall urban landscape. Natural increases in population through massive migration towards urban areas have created a variety of problems related to housing, education, health and employment. Consequently, the cities of Munger and Bhagalpur have experienced phenomenal rise in their residential areas.

The Sequence of People's Life and Culture

The development of urban culture is a stage of the sequence of social development. It is a corollary of food gathering, hunting, herding agricultural practices and urban development. According to Jacobi model, this has been linked with three-process e.g. domestication of plants and animals, the permanent cultivation of crops and the trading of goods with respect to urban centres. The position of these stages and processes with respect to the time is given along with the archaeological evidences.

Jacob's Model of Urban Cultural Development

Jane Jacob's emphasized the increasing evidence of highly specialized and long range among human populations are the forest gathering and hunting stage among cities of the historical past. Jocob's linear view of urbanization in terms of early trade and exchange and permanent agriculture decide the food requirements of the hybridized environment and quality of life of the urban people.

Huxley's Model of Culture

The British Biologist Julian Huxley had considered three parameters of culture while comparing cultural and biological evolution of man. The three components suggested are menti-facts, socio-facts and artifacts (Fig. 10.1).

Menti-Facts

These are considered in terms of religion, language, magic, folklore, artistic tradition and others. These are crucial and durable elements of culture, because they relate to human ability to think, to forge ideas and images against which other aspects of culture could be measured.

Socio-Facts

These aspects of culture create link between individual and groups as well. At individual level they include family structure, sexual behaviour and child rearing. At group level they include political and educational systems.

Artifacts

These are known as cultural freight of material manifestation of culture. These include group of material technology, e.g. food, shelter, transport, besides land utilization, crop production and design on the clothes are known as artifacts.

Levels of People's Life

The cities of Munger and Bhagalpur could be divided into three levels of quality of life.

(i) Central Business-*cum*-residential zone

(ii) Middle Residential *Mohallas*
(iii) Fringe Zone of Poor Peoples Home.

Central Business-cum-Residential Zone

This covers the fort of Munger and Champanagar in Bhagalpur, which stands on the southern natural levee of the Ganga River and effectively commanding the reaches of the river. Since long, the sites of these two cities have commanding position of considerable strategic importance. The British had acquired the Fort bazar estate for military purpose in 1770 A.D. Both remain under the commandant of the fort until 1840, when the bazar estate was handed over to the Civil authorities, but the fort was remain under the military authorities as a contonment until 1842. Currently, central businesses are of Munger and Bhagalpur is located out of this zone. The main roads of Munger come in this zone where Gola Bazar and Bekapur markets are located.

Middle Zone of Residential Mohallas

This zone covers residential *Mohallas* of the city. It covers the *Mohallas* of Chhoti Kelawari, Madhopur, Basudeopur, Raisar, Sandalpur, Ghositola, Shastrinagar and Chaintoli of Munger and Sahebganj, Tilka Manjhi, Parbati, Lalbag, Khanjarpur and Champanagar of Bhagalpur. In this area size of the wards are relatively bigger and the density of population is 5,000 persons per km^2.

Fringe Zone of Poor Peoples Home

In this area lowlying land, dump of urban refuge, poor peoples home due to low price of the land (Rs. 40,000) per katha and rise of slum, the general situations are not so attractive for the residents. It covers the intensive agricultural tracts of Laldarwaja, and Bank of Munger and Budhanath and Aliganj bus stand of Bhagalpur.

Changing Lifestyle in the Cities of Munger and Bhagalpur

A new affluence has crept up in the cities of Munger and Bhagalpur where people are spending a big amount of their budget for the purchase of jewellery, musical instruments and furring shoes that cost a month's salary'.

Most people in the cities of Munger and Bhagalpur live in tiny cramped houses that rarely have proper ventilation and 24 hours supply of running water. But in the cities like Munger and Bhagalpur most people owe colour television than can be operated by remote control. In this urban centre most of the families are now acquiring Video-cassette Recorders (VCR) which have become a status symbol of the quality of life.

A recent survey (2001) of households in the urban centres Munger and Bhagalpur by the census of India it has been revealed that out of every 1000 households, 60 have VCRs, 25 telephones, 15 air conditioners and 5 motor cars.

Most of the people considered for the sample survey owe a T.V., 25 per cent refrigerators and washing machines. In the urban centres of Munger and Bhagalpur a good doctor earns the *equivalent of a month salary in one-day* practice. In Indian situation the workers have no right to work at two places simultaneously even then the lifestyle of urbanites are quite different and found to be better in comparison with rural people in the surrounding country-side.

Bare cement floors and white washed walls are now being transferred to paints. Young peoples crage to buy the furniture's of different countries in their homes. The youth of Munger and Bhagalpur now described the changing life styles as 'interior decoration fever'. A survey revealed that urban families with per capita daily income of Rs. 130 spent on an average Rs. 2000 per month to decorate their homes.

Very recently, the excessive use of fashionable dresses especially by the college girls and computer revolution in day-to-day life have made the cultural advancement truly dynamic and ultra modern. Innovative street theatres are now commonly seen on festive occasions in the urban centres of Munger and Bhagalpur.

Change in the dress material could be seen as fore-fathers were wearing only one small piece of cloth in the year 1947 and now his grandson is wearing trouser, jacket, foreign made watches and play cricket game in place of *Kabadi*. This change could be observed normally in each and every family.

In olden days *Hukka* and *Chilam* were used for smoking and now cigarette has taken its place, in place of spear and farsa in the house pistol and gun has replaced, in place of oxen driven plough now the tractors are used, in place of bicycle now the scooters are coming on the scene of urban life of Munger and Bhagalpur. Before 1970 the tonga has been made out of used paper was very common but now polythene bags are used. During the past hearten hot prepared food was taken by the people but now the fast readymade food is taking place of the older ones.

Conclusion

This chapter is mainly related with types and patterns of urban peoples life with a view to analyse employment structure, income potential, caste and religious associations and act as nerve centre of political activities as well.

In the cities of Munger and Bhagalpur the patterns of urban life could be differentiated in terms of male and female living, rich and the poors lifestyle, labourers of a factory and rickshaw pullers, the *chanda* collection and begging alms, the unemployed and employed people, the pross and pandits, the politicians and the pleaders so on.

All these help in locating the quality of life of Hindu, Muslim, Christian, Sikh and Parsi as well. These variations are mainly due to religious differences and their customary behaviour. This also includes change in the patterns of living. Income differentials during past and the present and attainment in the level of education.

REFERENCES

Chatterjee, A.B. (1964), "Cultural History of Howrah City", *Geographical Review of India*; Vol. xxvl; pp. 23-24.

Dickinson, R.E. (1947), *City Region and Regionalism*, Routledge and Kegan Paul.

Fisher, C.S. (1975), "Towards Sub-cultural Theory and Urbanism", *American Journal of Sociology*, Vol. 80.

Lal, A.K. (1990), *The Urban Family*, Concept Publishing Company, New Delhi.

Mandal, R.B. (2000), *Urban Geography: A Text Book*, Concept Publishing Company, New Delhi, pp. 374-381.

Mumford, L. (1938), *The Culture of Cities*, Seeker and Warburg.

Nutgens, P.B.M. (1966), *Living in Towns*, B.B.C.

Self, P. (1961), *Cities in Flood*, Faber.

Sinha, S. (Eds.) (1972), *Cultural Profiles of Calcutta*, The Indian Anthropological Society, p. 283.

11 SUMMARY AND CONCLUSION

In this chapter measures have been adopted to deal with the variations in the quality of life of urban peoples in the cities of Munger and Bhagalpur. Such study has recently drawn attention of the scholars and the urban planners as well due to ever increasing population in the urban centres. This is wholly dependent on the person per room found in the residential house, types and patterns of latrines used by the urban resident, the level of literacy in per cent, the upkeep of lawns and gardens, dress materials, ornaments used and the food habit of people.

The quality of life is a conceptual view introduced recently by the Census of India (2001) in the State of Bihar. As the urban centres of Munger and Bhagalpur are the oldest one located in the Anga plain and hence, its historical development is chequerred but shrouds with mystry. Recently, the interplay of criminal gangs have created severe problems in the urban localities of Munger and Bhagalpur. It is amazing that the people of the cities have adopted modern way of living but the adoption level is very slow due to illiteracy, poverty and superstitiousness of residents of the locality or in the urban zone of influence.

In this project the interest has been shown that the people are keener in adopting modernity by the modern means of living but poverty is the main hurdle to have such a way of life. Cultural heritage is the guideline for the urbanites, and most of the people of Munger and Bhagalpur understand themselves as military might of the society as their forefathers have fought several wars with the kings and kingdoms who had putted their jealous eye of the administor of Anga.

The urban centres of Munger and Bhagalpur are located on latitude 25°N and longitude 86° and 87°E respectively in the Northern Hemisphere. These have been surrounded by the Ganga river from the north and the climate is drier east type due to annual rainfall of just 125 cm in the whole year. The vegetation is semi-dry monsoon type and the soil is coarse structure riverine sandy and loamy sand type. It comes under the levee zone of the Ganga river. The climate is salubrious and the land-use intensity is decreasing from central part of the cities towards its periphery due to distance decay function of population density, declining price of the land, gradient of population density and the safety of people from city core to the periphery.

The first chapter is devoted to introduction, i.e. significance of study of urban life, definition of the subject, scope and objectives of study, review of past literature on the subject, explanation of terminologies, methods of study, sources of data, hypothesis testing and geographical personality of the region. It could be hypothesized that urban life is the gift of physical and urban facilities available in the cities for the urban residents. At the end of this chapter the geographical personality of the urban centres of Munger and Bhagalpur has been analysed.

The second chapter is devoted to the ecological ground of the urban centres of Munger and Bhagalpur. This chapter explains the relief feature, climatic conditions, types and patterns of land-use, commercial agriculture of potato and vegetables, transportation linkages and the growth, distribution, density, sex ratio and future estimate of population. It has been observed the increment of urban population of Munger and Bhagalpur follows the path of geometric rate.

The third chapter is related with the factors such as relief, climate, vegetation, land utilization, crop production, industrial development, transport linkages and the concentration of people of different caste, religion, marital status and sex ratio in the urban centres of Munger and Bhagalpur where the urban way of living is more or less similar to other urban centres of the south Bihar Plain. Among the factors the effect of transport is most powerful in attracting people towards the cities of Munger and Bhagalpur from the surrounding hinterland.

The fourth and fifth chapter is associated with the formulation of conceptual models and view of the life of urban people of Munger and Bhagalpur. Under conceptual view it could be said that due to difference of rural and urban living the variations in life style, food habit, dress material, behaviour and peoples thinking are quite is closely related with agricultural seasons in terms of food, clothing and working hours but in urban it is more or less of similar nature throughout the year. Hence, the urban life is more artificial and rural living is guided by the natural phenomena.

The sixth chapter is related with the types and patterns of urban peoples life in relation to employment structure, income potential, caste and religious affinity and act as never centre of political activities in the urban centre.

- Urban Life
  - Rich People
    - Marwaris
    - Business Class
  - Middle Income Group People
    - Contractors
    - Service Class
  - Low Income Group People
    - Menials
    - Labourers

The pattern of urban life could be differentiated with the help of male and female living conditions, rich and poor. The sample study is given in seventh chapter, which has been based at family; occupation, income, caste and various process of urban life have been considered. The seventh chapter is devoted to in frastructural development in the cities of Munger and Bhagalpur in terms of road development of educational institutions. Lifestyle, labourers of a factory and rickshaw pullers, the *Chanda* business and the beggars, the unemployed people and the service class people, the pandits and the pross, the politicians and the pleaders and so on.

The eighth chapter is devoted to measure the level of quality of urban peoples life in true to the sense. In reality in the urban centres of Munger and Bhagalpur there is only the distribution of poverty and everywhere people live in dilapidated buildings admist filth and dirt. The poverty, illiteracy, ignorance and urban misery are the causes of wretched quality of life found in the urban centres of Munger and Bhagalpur. An average German says that 'only poors are living in India. You Indians you are eating too much that's why you are poor'. The littered household items, no bed sheet on the cot, unfiltered drinking water, and travelling along distance by the students of boys and girls for going to school are some of the measuring rods of quality of life found in the State of Bihar.

In ninth chapter discussions have been made regarding the problems of poverty, misery, slum development, road holds up by the thieves burglary, theft, flood, drought and vice of the underworlds are rampant issues affecting the quality of life in urban areas. Among the prospects hope for the better life, planned development of colonies and relocation and remodelling of slums, respite form the various kinds of diseases, supply of safe drinking water and the control of excessive population growth through preventive methods of family planning. The robbery on roads, killing spree by the revolutionary's should immediately be stopped.

The sample study is given in seventh chapter which has been based at family occupation, income, caste and various processes of urban life have been considered. The eighth chapter is devoted to infrastructural development in the cities of Munger and Bhagalpur in terms of road network, housing and the supply of drinking water and electricity and the development of educational institutions.

The last chapter is on summary and conclusions, which shows the urban life of the people of Munger and Bhagalpur. At the end, this may be said that the urban life of Munger and Bhagalpur is not so congenial due to eruption of various problems in the society created by the insurgencies, poverty and non-cooperation of people with the government machinery.

Conclusions

The urban area is not only the resultant of wider processes, it in turn generates its own social force. Imagine a meeting in an inner city area, which has just been the scene of violence and loot. The people in the room will see quite different images of the urban. The representative of one of the looted chain stores will be considering the level of his losses, the problem of increasing insurance premiums and the possibility of shifting his investment elsewhere. The planner will think of the physical fabric and have in mind her plan for refurnishing and redevelopment. She will be aware of the crumbling facades, the decaying infrastructure of sewers and roads, and the need of more investment. The social worker will think of the area as the source of a heavy load of cases. He will think of individuals and families struggling to cope with too little money and little likelihood that thing will get better. An industrialist, encouraged to attend the meeting by some powerful person outside the area, who sees it as an area of low skills, possible labour militancy and a difficult site to develop, involving an awkward journey to work for his managers. It would not be difficult to imagine the thoughts of the other people who might be at such a meeting—the local general practitioners, or those anxious to excavate 'the medieval core of the city,' the local councillors and local MPs concerned about being re-elected, the chief of police for the area, community workers and clergyman, housing managers and representatives from the Trades Council and the Rotary

Club, youth workers and leaders of other youth organizations, teachers and representatives of the Education Department, local dignitatries—magistrates, landowners of those with 'family connections' in the area or those associated with housing association — local political activists, students and researchers. The list could easily and plausibly be extend for another page and in no case would it be difficult to imagine what is likely to be in the minds of those living there. Let us assume we have got all these different views, fears, ideas, fallacies, misconceptions and insights in our head. We may then remember that not one of the people need necessarily live in the area in question. The clergyman is most likely to do so and the business leaders and dignitaries least likely to. If we have successfully understood not only what is in the minds of all these people, but also the degree of power and influence they have severally and collectively to affect what goes on in this city, we will, of course, know a great deal. This Project may help to structure an understanding of the forces and processes that such people represent. We can understand how the household, which is a cause for concern to the social worker is seen by the employer as simply unkilled labour, probably un-employable.

However, if all we see is so many roles, positions, institutions structures and processes, we may end up with much knowledge and little understanding. We can provide systematic accounts derived from knowledge of housing tenure, local authority committee minutes, returns made to the Department of Employment or whatever: such exercises in abstraction have inevitably taken us a long way from the kerb level. If we return to our meeting, there is surely something a little odd about our account which focused on all the officials and representatives of this and that had nothing at all to say about what was in the heads of the people who were at the meeting — simply because they lived in the area and for no other reason. It would be a curious sociology, which described the ideologies of the management, ignored the workers and then claimed that this was an adequate basis for knowledge of the structures and processes of industrial life. Clearly, the actual experience of industrial or urban life by those who are most disadvantaged cannot be distilled from an accumulation of professionals' partial perspectives, description of housing markets, labour markets and different kinds of work sets the scene but does not bring the play to life.

People's experience of the place they live in comes from what they actually experience in the events of their ordinary everyday life.

The familiar faces of their local social networks help to structure their experience. They see programmes on TV in the context of their families and the friends they meet in pubs or outside the school gates. Their experience of wage labour is in the context of the others they share the experience with. Their expectation of work is mediated to them by what they first hear from their families and friends. People are conscious of the history of the place they live in, even when most landmarks to their past are destroyed. Famous football teams, a work that once dominated an area, the 'local' pub, familiar streets, bus routes acid faces all give style and a particular feel to a place. Moving to another city of another part of the same city breaks the continuity until a new set of social landmarks emerges.

We have emphasised the constraints of housing and labour markets, the dominaton of a 'formal' urban system and the gatekeepers who control access to a whole range or urban resources and facilities. This approach makes 'the urban' appears as a set of forces which weigh upon the people. The local state, the police, the welfare state, the enabling professions handle their clients, cases, patients, applicants, claimants, kids, youth, old people and problems of all descriptions. But of course we know that when we talk of "the managing of everyday life" we are referring primarily to the management of people who have little else but the capacity to sell their labour power for a wage. Some of the chapters were about the structure and processes of urban life that dominate ordinary working people.

We thus come to a curious paradox. Thoughout much of urban life the city dweller or citizen was distinct from ordinary working people and it is they who are the typical urban dwellers. The contemporary bourgeois are more likely to live in suburbs or outside the cities and those living in the centre at least have a 'weekend cottage' to which they can retreat. So, in Munger and Bhagalpur the basis of working class culture has become urban. Unlike countries, which have urbanised later, like France or even the United States, the English working class does not have a peasant or small town background to provide a sort of cultural datum. This is not to say that rural type activities such as keeping pigeons or perrets are not common, but they are definitely rural type pursuits or urban people.

Urban sociologists are returning to the study of detailed ethnography of local populations after a decade or more of neglect. Stimulated by the ideas of the Birmingham centre for Contemporary Cultural Studies, a new generation of researchers is less prepared to accept overly structural determination of people's activities. They are reacting to a kind of sociology, which was fashionable in the mid-1970s, which left people as puppets bobbing up and down to the strings of monopoly apitalism and the 'oppressive state apparatus'. We do not dispute that the way our society works it constraining and dominating for most ordinary people. The work they do demands little skill and responsibility and is frequently noisy, dirty and even dangerous. Huge lorries thunder through city streets and the visual environment of the 'paradises' of shops in the suburbs or the heap of super markets in centres is often squalid and degrading. Council estates give drab and dreary impression, in marked contrast to the diversity and interest often found in middle class suburbs. But, having said that, we return to our opening sentence. People are not crushed into passive submission. They create their own worlds despite the enveloping structures and processes we have described. People make their own history and their own urban life, which has not made for them.

The curious thing is that although sociologists recognise the distinctiveness and importance of working-class culture, they have been slower to come to a deeper understanding of it than other matters one thing is, however, very clear that there is no single working-class culture which unites ordinary working people. There are distinctive working-class cultures which are local and who have been tied to places and regions. The nature and range of jobs that have been and are available is of crucial importance. Working-class consciousness on fringe is tied to the experiences; different forms of conflict or incorporation and different employment opportunities produce distinctive responses. In areas which have not been dominated by a single employer or industry, other social elements provide continuity with a long and varied history of stable and diverse employment. A working-class population can get well noted in an area. Generations go to school together and are not obliged to leave the area to find employment. So they marry locally and attend each other's weddings. Family events become community events; the local paper telling of births, deaths and marriages provides the most salient news. The faces in the pubs, the church halls jumble sales and the cafes are familiar. Local social networks are tightly enmeshed and, since women typically control the power based on kin, they may feel, and indeed be, less powerless than in newly settled areas.

The distinctive cultural practices of working-class life do not wobble about according to the fads and fashions of the mass media, as some would argue. This is because the experience is mediated through a local context and, by definition; the mass media cannot cover the whole range of distinctiveness.

(a) Material conditions of the given social formation in the	1. Job markets 2. Housing markets 3. Formal Urban	1.The context of urban life 2. Community sources of conscious	Working Class Cultural Practies and Orginisation
(b) The specific history of employment and political activity		3. Patterns of demographic change and stability.	

Experiences and context at the same time. Hence, there is generally a disjunction between the general and the specific or the national and the local way of life. Overwhelmingly, working-class life is family life and such life has to be lived in specific contexts. If the knowledge about markets and bureaucracies is to develop into understanding, then it must be put into a local context of distinctive working-class cultural practices. This must involve a substantial amount of historical knowledge and understanding of ethnic differences and practices. Other local symbols than pub or chapel have to be incorporated into such an understanding. In the same way, that it is misleading to view the working-class through the eyes of male chief earners, so it is equally misleading to view it entirely through the eyes of white Anglo-Saxons.

Our cities and cities will change over the next few decades and hence urban history confirms that urban change and conflict is the normal expectation. This change will not be a mechanistic one-way flow from the structure of markets to the families who are submissively acted upon. Rather, we must recognise that people play a part in creating their own history; working-class consciousness and political action emerge from distinctive contexts.,

It is arguable that the local contexts well have greater salience in the 1980s than it had in the middle of the century when employment was such a distinctive determinant of life-chances. As formal employment declines, and as disliking of male manual workers continues, it is increasingly implausible to see the link between the household and the economy as being based entirely on the occupation of the male chief earner. Whom you know well.

Urban Life Itself is a Product of the Historical Context

Urban life itself is a product of a given set of historical circumstances. The concepts and ideas which hold strongest away at a particular time are those that best fit the immediate material circumstances. And evidently these changes, which we have seen the how Chicago in the 1920s was the scene for the development of a distinctive ecological approach. This was associated with a rapidly expanding capitalism, which provided the motor for change in the Central Business District, which expanded into the zone of transition. Similarly, the waves of new and diverse migrants into the city did much to produce its mosaic of social worlds.

In Britain in the 1960s, by contrast, the welfare state was rapidly expanding in all directions. Perhaps not surprisingly, this was the era of 'urban managerialism' which carried on to the mid-1970s. The focus was then on the constraining power of bureaucracies and their agents. The 'gate keepers' still prominently in this thesis.

However, towards the middle of the 1970s it becomes clear that 'the urban fiscal crisis' was not to be explained by the style of managers. By analogy, that would imply that when a firm closed down as a result of a change in world market conditions it would be appropriate to blame the personnel manager. Evidently, the asset-stripping boom of the early 1970s was following a logic, which produced greater profit from land and property than from labour and manufacturing. The growth of multinational companies and the takeover of much of British industry by external capital led to an awareness of the broader structural forces which could not be controlled locally. Perhaps the most symbolic and significant example of this process was the dramatic increase in oil prices after 1973. So urban sociology in the 1970s inevitably became more concerned with the climate and less concerned with the pool, to revert to our previous analogy. Probably, the most influential bood of this period was 'The Urbane Question by Manuel Castells', although many people found it easier to approach his ideas through his commentators and critics, such as C.G. Pickvance and Peter Saunders. Those who are stimulated by this book to deepen their understanding of the field will find Peter Saunder's book, Social Theory and the Urban Question (1981), a most valuable guide to debates, which are not appropriately considered here.

However, the urban sociology of the 1980s will be different again form that of the 1960s and the 1970s. The shift from managerialism to structuralism did not fit the decades as closely as that and the pivotal years were more likely 1967, when Race, Community and Conflict was published, and the mid-1970s, when the so-called was published, and the mid-1970s, when the so-called 'new' urban sociology had its heyday. The International journal of Urban and Regional Research, which serves as a focus for much of the more radical New York, began in 1977 and reflects the substantial shift of thinking over the previous decade. In 1981 this Journal published a powerful article by Professor Ivan Szelenyi of the University of Wisconsin, who is one of the most creative urban sociologists of his generation in the world. He argued that the wave of the new urban sociology of the 1970s based on structuralism was now over. It had served its purpose in the material circumstances of the time, but now there was a need to face a new agenda with different questions. He, too, reacted against the over-determinism of previous years and directed thinking towards new areas, such as the domestic/informal economy or the distinctiveness of urban life under socialism.

We argue, therefore, that it is important to put ideas in context, what counts as 'urban for urban geographers' will charge over time as the arguments and intellectual focus also change. We suggest that a greater concern with how ordinary people 'get by' will come to have more salience as structural unemployment makes its impact through the 1980s. The insights generated during earlier debates will still inform those debtes which are yet to come, but as the material circumstances change, so too, will concepts and ideas. We see these theses less as a review of a body of knowledge, which is firmly, established, but rather more an introduction to a way of looking at the structures and processes of urban life.

Munger and Bhagalpur were the cities to cope with the problem of urban-industrial society. Yet even by the last decades of the nineteenth century Munger and Bhagalpur starting to lose her industrial pre-eminence. Economists now talk about de-industrialisation as a process, which can be subscribed and understood.

We have not yet started to talk about de-industrialisation in the same way. However, as the material forces which produced huge new industrial complexes and the urban infrastructure to support them change, so too must the contexts. How the work is done and who does it may have to change. The impact of this on urban life may well be the theme for the coming wave of urban social theory. So theory and practice will interrelate in a neve-ending dialectic. The structures and processes of urban life in the 1980s change but their style of interaction will remain the same. Such is the paradox of urban life in almost all the cities.

BIBLIOGRAPHY

Abrams, C. (1953), Urban Land Problems and Policies; *Housing, Town and Country Planning, Bulletin* 7, UNO.

Abrams, P. and Wrigley, E.A. (eds.) (1974), *Towns in Societies,* Cambridge University Press.

Achuta Rao, T.N. (1967), The Concept of Twin Towns, *Geographical Review of India*, Vol. 29, pp. 104-107.

Ahmad, E. (1956), Origin and Evaluation of Towns of Uttar Pradesh; *Geographical Outlook*, Vol. 1, pp.38-58.

Ahmad, S. (1950), *Dacca : A Study in Urban History and Development*, Curzon Press, London.

Alden, H. (1977), 'The extent an nature of double job holding in Great Britain', *Industrial Relations Journal* (B) 3, 1977, pp.14-31.

Alexander, F.G. and Selesnick, S.T. (1996), *The History of Psychology*. New York, Harper and Row.

Anderson, M. (1971), *Family Life in Nineteenth Century Lancashire*, Cambridge University Press.

Anal, S.K. Singh (1980), *Origin and Growth of Towns*, Concept Publishing Co., New Delhi.

Ashworth, William (1954), *The Genesis of Modern British Town Planning*, Routledge.

Barron, R.D. and Morris, G.M. (1976), ' Sexual divisions and the dual labour market' in Barker, D.L. and Allen, S. (eds), *Dependence and Exploitation in Work and Marriage*, Longman, London.

Baum, A. (1998), Disasters, natural and otherwise, *Psychology Today*, 22 pp. 56-60.

Bandura, A. (1973), *Aggression : A Social Learning Analysis*. Englewood Cliffs, N.J. Printice-Hall.

Beckinsale, R.P. and Houseton, J.M. (1968), *Urbanization and Its Problems*; Backwall.

Berry, B.J. (1968), 'Theories of Urban Location', *Annals of the Association of American Geographers*, Resource Paper I, Washington.

Berkman, L.F. and Syme, S.L. (1979), Social Networks, Host Resistance and Mortality : A nine-year follow-up study of Alameda County residents. *American Journal of Epidemiology*, 109. 186-204.

Bhatt, L.S. *et al.* (1976), *Micro Level Planning*, K.B. Publications, New Delhi.

Blackburn, R.M. and Mann, M. (1979), *The Working Class in the Labour Market*, Macmillan, London.

Boal, F.W. Murray, R.C. and Poole, M.A. (1976), 'Belfast: the urban encapsulation of a national conflict' in Glass, S.C. and Obler, J.L. (eds.) *Urban Ethnic Conflict: A Comparative Perspective*, University of North Carolina, Chapel Hill,

Briggs, Asa, (1968), *Victorian Cities* (rev.edn.), Penguin Books.

Bruse, G. and Whitemen, D.F. (1953), *An Approach to Urban Planning,* Princeton University Press.

Burgess, E.W. (1925), 'The growth of the city' in Park, R.E. *et al. The City,* University of Chicago Press (Reprinted 1967).

Buckley, W. (1967), *Sociology and Modern System Theory*, Englewood Cliffs, New Jersey, Prentice Hall.

Castells, M. (1977), *The Urban Question*, Edward Arnold.

Castells, M. (1977), 'Towards a Political Urban Sociology', In Harloe, M. (ed.) *Captive Cities*, John Wiley.

CDP (1977), *The Costs of Industrial Change*, Inter Project Editorial Team, London.

Centre for Contemporary Cultural Studies, University of Birmingham; Resistance Through Rituals, 1976.

Chand, Mahesh and Vishwakarma, R.K. (1972), "Urbanization as a Strategy of Rural Development", *Urban Systems and Rural Development*, Mysore, p.141.

Charistall, W. (1965), *Central Places in Southern Germany,* Englewood Cliff.

Chatterjee, A.B. (1964), 'Cultural History of Howrah City', *Geographical Review of India*, XXVI, pp. 23-24.

Charmers, T. (1820), *The Christian and Civic Economy of Large Towns*, 3 Vols. London.

Christaller, W. (1966) *Central Places in Southern Germany*. Prentice Hall, New Jersey, p. 64.

Clark, Collin (1951), "Urban Population Densities", *Journal of Statistical Society*, Vol. 1, pp. 492-596.

Clark, P. and Slack, P. *English Towns in Transition*, Oxford, 1500-1700.

Cobb, S. (1976), Social Support as a Moderator of Life Stress. *Psychosomatic Medicine*, **38**, 300-314.

Cohan, S. (1978), Environmental load and allocations of attentions, in A. Baum. J.E. Singer and S. Valins (Eds.), *Advances in Environmental Psychology* (Vol. I, pp. 1-29), Hillsdale, NJ: Erlabaum.

Creson, M. (1971), *The UN-Politics of Air Pollution*, John Hopkins Press, Baltimore.

Darner, S. (1976), 'A note on housing allocation' in Edwards, M. *et al.* (eds) *Housing and Class in Britain Conference of Socialist Economists*, London.

Davies, J.O. and Taylor, J. (1970), 'Race, Community and no convict', *New Society*, 16, pp. 67-69.

Dear, M. and Scott, A.J. (eds.), (1981), *Urbanisation and Urban Planning in Capitalist Society,* Methuen.

Dearlove, J. (1973), *The Politics to Policy in Local Government,* Cambridge, University Press.

Desai, A.P. (1982), *The Indian City: A Conformation of Culture, Ibid.,* 1982, p. 148.

Dixon-Mueller, R. and Wateriest, J. (1991), The Culture of Silence : Reproductive Tract Infections among woman in the Third world. *International Women's Health Coalition*, New York.

Dhabriya, S.S. (1964), 'Evolution of Cultural Landscape in Udaipur City'. *National Geographical Journal of India*, Vol, 10, pp. 92-99.

Donnison, D. (1981), Cite in Trouble, University of Glasgow, Centre for Urban and Regional Studies, *Discussion Paper* No. 39.

Donnison, D. and Soto, P. (1980), *The Good City: A Study of Urban Development and Policy in Britain*, Heinemann Educational, London.

Dunleavy, P. (1980), *Urban Political Analysis*, Macmillan.

Dunleavy, P. (1979), 'The urban basis of political alignment', *British Journal of Political Science*, 9, 1979, pp. 409-43.

Dyos, H.J. (1968), (ed.) The Study of Urban History, Edward Arnold.

Ellefesen, R.A. (1962), 'City Hinterland Relationship in India,' in *India's Urban Future*, Oxford University Press, Bombay.

Engels, F. (1895), *The Condition of the Working Class in England.*

Foster, J. (1974), *Class Struggle and the Industrial Revolution*, Methuen.

Friedman (1966), "Two Concepts of Urbanizations: A Comment", *Urban Affairs Quarterly*, 1, 1966, p. 80.

Fitzherbert, A. (1958), *After Industrial Society's The Emerging Self-service Economy*, Macmillan.

Frodler, J.L. (1981), "A review of the literature on access and utilization of medical care with special emphasis rural primary care". *Social Science and Medicine* 50 : 129-142.

Gandhi, Indira (1975), 'Haphazard Growth of our Cities', *Yojana*, Vol. XIX, No. 15, November 1975, pp. 5-8.

Geyer, H.S. and Kontuly, T.M. *Differential Urbanization Peoples Response to Quality of Life*, *Ibid.*, p. 20.

Gershuny, J. and Thomas, G., Changing Patterns of Time Use, Science Policy Research Unit, University of Sussex, Occasional Paper No. 20.

George, M. Dorothy (1965), *London Life in the Eighteenth Century,* Penguin 'First Published Kegan Paul, Trench, Trubner, 1925 and 1965.

Glass, R. (1968), 'Urban Sociology in Great Britain' in Pahl, R.E. (ed.), *Readings in Sociology*, Pergamons Press.

Gopalkrishnan, K.S. (1992), *Sustainable Quality of Life and the Metropolie*, *Ibid.,* p. 223.

Grimm, F. (1979), *The Settlement System of the GDR*. Leipzig.

Haddon, R. (1970), 'A Minority in the Welfare State', *New Atlantis*, 2, pp. 80-123.

Hall, P. Grace, H. Dewitt, R. and Thomas, R. (1973), *The Containment of Urban England*, Allen and Unwind.

Harvey, D. (1973), *Social Justice and the City*, Edward Arnold.

Hatt, P.K., Reiss, J. and Albert, Jr. (1963), *Cities and Society*, The Free Press of Glencoe, Inc, New York.

Harloe, M. Swindon (1975), *A Town in Transition*, Heinemann.

Harloe, M. and Lebas, E. (eds), (1981), *City, Class and Capital,* Edward Arnold.

Harrel, J.P. (1980), Psychological factors and hypertension : A status report. *Psychological Bulletin*, 87, 482-501.

Home and Community in English Society in Mitchell, J. and Oakley, A. (eds.), *The Rights and Wrongs of Woman*, Penguin, 1986.

Hosilitz, B.F. (1959), Cities of India and Their Problems; *Annals of the Association of Americal Geographers*, Vol. 49, pp. 223-231.

Huda, Z., Hind, K. Nabil, Y. El. Monselhy, M. and Mohamed Fadle, (1993), "Concepts and measure of reproductive morbidity. *Health Transition Review. The Cultural, Social and Behavioural Determinants of Health*. Vol. 3, No. 1.

Hutchinson (1980), *Working Class Culture, Media, Language,* Hutchinson, 1979.

Illich, I. *The Right of Useful Unemployment*, Marion Bayars.

Illich, I. (1981), *Shadow Work*, Marion Bayars.

Illich, I. (1978), *The Right to Useful Unemployment,* Marion Bayars.

Jefferson, M. 'The Distribution of the World City Folks: A Study in Comparative Civilization', *Geographical Review*, Vol. 21, p.453.

Johnson, J. (1972), *Professions and Power*, Macmillan, London.

Johnson, T.J. (1977), "What is to be known"? *Economy and Society*, 6, pp. 194-233.

Krantz, D.S. *et al.* (1987), Stress and Type a Behaviour : Interactions between environmental and biological factors. In A. Baum and J.E. Singer (Eds.) *Hardware of Psychology and Health* (Vol.5), Hillsdate, N.J. Eribaum.

Krecked, R. (1980), 'Unequal Opportunity Structure and Labour Market segmentation', *Sociology*, 14, 1980, pp. 525-50.

Kroger. A. (1983), 'Anthropological and socio-medical health care research in developing countries'. *Social Science and Medicine* 17 (3) : 147-161.

Lai, A.K. (1992), *Urban Family: A Study of Hindu Social Systems,* Concept Publishing Co., New Delhi.

Lambert, J., Paris, C. and Blackaby, B. (1978), *Housing Policy and the State,* Macmillan, London.

Lambert, C and Weir, D. (eds.), (1975), *Cities in Modern Britain,* Fontand.

Lansley, S. (1979), *Housing and Public Policy*, Croom Helm, London.

Losch, A. (1954), *Economics of Location*, Yale University Press.

Lowenstein, S.F. (1965), Urban Images of Roman authors, *Comparative Studies in Society and History*, 8, 1965, pp. 110-23.

Lukes, S. Power (1974), *A Radical View,* Macmillan.

Mallick, U.C. (1979), 'Development of Small Towns for Balanced Urbanization and Economic Growth', *Place of Small Towns in India*, Varanasi, p. 55.

Mandal, R.B. (1982), *Land Utilization: Theory and Practice,* Concept Publishing Co. New Delhi, p. 76.

Margulis, H.L. *East Asian Villages and Downtrodden Development, Ibid.*, p. 395.

Marshall, J.D. (1968), 'Colonisation as a Factor in the Planning of Towns in Northwest England' in Dyos, *op. cit.*

Martin, R. and Fryer, R.H. (1973), *Redundancy and Paternalist Capitalism*, George Allen and Unwin, London.

Meacham, S.A. (1977), *Life Apart: The English Working Class 1890-1914.* Thames and Hudson.

McCraken, K.W.J. *Methods of Need Assessment for Community Human Services Planning.*

Mellor, R. (1977), *Urban Sociology in an Urbanised Society,* Routledge and Kegan Paul.

Mishra, H.N. (1992), *Quality of Life in Squatter Settlements,* Allahabad, p. 421.

Mullu, T.A. 'Working Life as a Part of Personal Welfare in Finland: A Regional Approach', *Ibid.,* p. 437.

Murie, A. Niner, P. and Wetson, C. (1976), *Housing Policy and the Housing System,* George Allen and Unwin.

Murphy, R. (1969), 'Traditional and Coloinialism; Changing Urban Roles in Asia', *Journal of Asian Studies*, Vol. 29, pp. 67-84.

Nath, U. (1962), 'The Village and the Community', Edited by Roy Turner, in *India's Urban Future,* University of California Press, pp. 151-153.

Norris, G.M. (1978), 'Unemployment, Sub-employment and Personal Characteristics'. *The Sociological Review,* 26, pp. 89-108, and pp. 327-47.

Norris, G.M. (1978), 'Industrial Paternalist Capitalism and Local Labour Markets' *Sociology* (12). 3, 1978, pp. 469-89.

Newton, K. (1976), *Second City Politics,* Oxford University Press.

Okamoto, K. (1979), *The Quality of Life in Metropolitan Suburbs of Japan*, p. 471.

Open University Course D. 202, *Urban Change and Conflict,* 1982.

Pahl, R.E. *et al.* (1975), *Structure and Process of Urban Life,* Longman, London.

Pahl, R.E. (1979), 'Socio-Political Factors in Resource Allocation', Chapter 3 in Herbert, D.T., Smith, D.M. (eds.), *Social Problems and the City,* Oxford University Press.

Pahl, R.E. (1981), 'Employment Work and the Domestic Division of Labour' in Harloe, M. and Lebas, F. (eds.), *City, Class and Capital: New Developments in the Political Economy of Cities and Regions,* Edward Arnold.

Pahl, R.E. (1983), 'Concepts in Contexts: Pursuing the "Urban" Sociology' in D. Fraser and A Sutcliffe (eds.) *The Pursuit of Urban History,* Edward Arnold.

Pirenne, H. (1956), *Medieval Cities* (New Pub.), Doubleday, Anchor Books, Sjoberg' *The Preindustrial City,* The Free Press of Glencoe, 1960.

Phythian-Adams, C. (1978), 'Urban decay in late Medieval England' in P. Abrams and E.A. Wrigley (eds.) *op. cit*, pp.159-86.

Phythian-Adams, C. (1978) 'Ceremony and the citizen: The Communal Year at Covernry 1450-1550' in Clark, Rand Slack, P. (eds.) *Crisis and Order in English Towns 1500-1700*, London, pp. 57-85.

Pickvance, C.G. (1976), (ed.) *Urban Sociology: Critical Easays*, Tavistock.

Pickvance, C.G. (1981), 'Policies as Chameleons: Regional and Office Policy in Britain' in Dear, M.J. and Scott, A. (eds.), *Urbanisation and Urban Planning in Capitalist Societies,* Methuen, London.

Pickvance, C .G. (1977), ' Marxist approaches to the Study of Urban Politics: Devergences among some recent French Studies', *International Journal of Urban and Regional Research,* pp. 219-55.

Prasad, S.D. (1961), Census of India, Part 1 (A) General Report on the Census, p. 151.

Prient, R.G. (1998), 'Benzodiazepines : The search for tranquillity', in M.J. Chrisbel and P.G. Mellett (Eds.), *The Psychosonation Approach : Centemporary Practice of Whole,* Person Care, New York: Willey.

Peveler, R.C. and Johnston, D.W. (1986) Subjective and cognitive effects of relaxation, *Behaviour Research and Therapy*, 24, 413-419.

Raju, S. 'Access of the Urban Poor to Basic Anenities in Delhi', India, *Ibid.*, p. 521.

Reeve, S.A. (1917), 'Congestion in Cities', *Geographical Review,* pp. 278-293.

Resenstock, E. (1966), "Child mortality and fertility in Columbia: Individual and community effects", *Health Policy and Education*, Vol. 2, 385.

Rex, J. and Moore, R. (1967), *Race, Community and Conflict*, Oxford University Press, London.

Roberts, R. (1973), *The Classic Slum*, Penguin.

Rule, J. (1981), *The Experience of Labour in the Eighteenth Century*, Croom Helm.

Saunder, P. (1979), *Urban Politics: A Sociological Interpretation*, Hutchinson.

Sundaram, K.V. (1972), "Growth of the Urban Economy of Small and Medium Sized Towns", in *Urban and Regional Planning in India*, Vikas Publishing House Pvt. Ltd, New Delhi, p. 213.

Saunders, P. (1981), *Social Theory and the Urban Question*, Hutchinson.

Selye, H. (1976). *The Stress of Life* (Revised Edition) New York: Mc Graw-Hill.

Shadiro. J.L. (1987), The expectant father. *Psychology Today*, 21, pp. 36-42.

Shepherd, J., Westaway, J. and Lee, T. (1974), *A Social Atlas of London*, Oxford University Press.

Singh, B. *National Capital Region and Eco-Environmental Hazards*, *Ibid.*, p. 580.

Stedman Jones, G. 'Working Class—Culture and Working Class Politics in London 1870-1900', *Journal of Social History*, 8, pp. 460-508.

Szelenyi, I. (1981), 'Structural changes of and alternatives to Capitalist Development in the Contemporary Urban and Regional System', *International Journal of Urban and Regional Research* (5), 1, pp. 1-14.

Tacitus (trans. 1948) *On Britain and Germany* (trans. H. Mattingley), Penguin Books.

Thieme, G.H. (1948), *Quality of Life and Mortality: The German Example*, p. 614.

Thompson. P. The Edwardians Weidenfeld and Nicholson Tilly, L.A. and Scott, J.W. (1978), *Women, Work and Family*, Holt, Rinehart and Winston.

Thrupp, Sylvia L. (1962), *The Merchant Class of Medieval London*, University of Michigan Press, An Arbon Paperback.

UNICEF (1989). *State of the World's Children 1989*. Oxford University Press, New York.

Vooged, H. (1992), 'Quality of Life and Images: Some Methodological Issue', *Abstract of 27th International Geographical Congress*, Washington, p. 653.

Ward, R.H. (1978), "Race Relation in Britain", *British Journal of Sociology*, 29, 1978, p. 4.

Weber, A. F. (1899), *The Growth of Cities in the Nineteenth Century*; reprint edn. Cornell Paperbacks (OUP).

Weber, M. (1958), *The City*, Heinemann (First Published in German).

Weber, M.J. (1969), "Sub-Optional Behaviour and the Concept of Maximum Profits in Location Theory", *Australian Geographical Studies*, 7, 1969, p. 1.

Willams, O.P. (1971), *Metropolitan Political Analysis*, Free Press, New York.

Willams, R. 'The Country and the City', Chatto and Windus Wrigley, E.A. (1978) 'A Simple Model of London's Improtance in Changing English Society and Economy 1650-1750' in Abrms, P. and Wrigley, E.A. *op. cit.* pp. 215- 44.

White, J. Rothschild (1980), *Buildings: Life in an East and Tenement Block 1877-1920*, Routledge and Kegan Paul.

Wese, M.J. (1964), Problems and Planning of Changing Britain; *Geography*, Vol. 49.

Yadav, C.S. (eds) (1992), *Slums, Urban Decline and Revitalization*, Concept Publishing Company, New Delhi.

Zimbardo, P.G. (1988). *Psychology and Life* (12th ed.) Glenview, IL: Scott, Foreman.

Zorbauah, H.W. (1929), *The Gold Coast and the Slum*, Chicago University Press.

INDEX